Ghost Cats 2

More Afterlife Encounters with Feline Spirits

ALSO FROM STUPID GRAVITY PRESS

Ghost Cats: Human Encounters with Feline Spirits

Cat Scene Investigator: Solve Your Cat's Litter Box Mystery

Finding Your Missing Cat: The Practical Cat-Specific Guide for Your Happy Reunion

Praise for Ghost Cats 2

"Well-written, thoughtful and insightful. This book provides further understanding of our furry feline friends both in the physical and spirit form." –Phyllis Galde, publisher of *Fate Magazine* and *Species Link Journal*

"Sometimes funny, sometimes chilling. Always comforting visitations of our cats from beyond the grave." –Carole Nelson Douglas, author of the *Midnight Louie* mystery series

"A fascinating book, whether you're a skeptic or a believer." –Dr. Marty Becker, America's Veterinarian

"*Ghost Cats 2* encounters run the gamut of human emotions: from unsettling to funny to comforting. This book has a feline phantom for everyone." –*Catster*

"A thoroughly captivating read that leaves one wanting a third book. But be warned, not all the spirits that grace these pages are benevolent, or feline!" –Andrea Dorn, award-winning writer

"The perfect gift for anyone who has loved and lost a cat." –Clea Simon, author of *A Cat on the Case*, a *Witch Cat of Cambridge* mystery

"Funny and terrifying. A completely satisfying insight into the magnitude of the human-feline bond." –Mollie Hunt, author of *Crazy Cat Lady Mystery* series

"An outstanding gem in the literature not just of departed pets, but of the transcendent realm, for all of us." –Mary A. Turzillo, *Cosmic Cats & Fantastic Furballs*

"*Ghost Cats 2* made a believer out of me." –Marci Kladnik, past president, Cat Writers' Association, and author of the *Maggie and Barney* children's book series

"*Ghost Cats 2* is comfort soup for all cat owners who miss their special feline. Insightful and positively written, it entertains and assures the reader one day they will all meet again." –Heike Hagenguth, award-winning cat writer, Cairo, Egypt

"Cat lovers will find this a purr-fect read, one that will give them hope that they, too, may one day experience a visit from their own lost pets." –Debbie De Louise, author of the award-winning *Cobble Cove* cozy mystery series

"*Ghost Cats 2* is a must read!" –Arden Moore, author of *The Cat Behavior Answer Book*

"An engaging and reassuring look at how feline guardian angels bring comfort to their loved ones after crossing the Rainbow Bridge." –Barbara Bullington, School of Communication, East Carolina University

"This was so fun to read! A su-purr-lative & spook-tacular read you can really knead your paws into." –Cassandra Morgan, president of Cat Writers' Association and author of *The Kingdoms of Chartile*

"Lovely accounts of people and their fur babies, their fur babies' spirits, and their fur babies' souls." –Shawn P. Flynn, award-winning author of *THE KITTY Who Rescued Me After I Rescued Him*

Ghost Cats 2

More Afterlife Encounters with Feline Spirits

Dusty Rainbolt

Stupid Gravity Press, LLC
Lewisville, Texas

Ghost Cats 2: More Afterlife Encounters with Feline Spirits

Dusty Rainbolt
Copyright © 2022 by Dusty Rainbolt
Copy editor, Beth Adelman
Illustrations by Stephanie Piro
Proofreaders: Marci Kladnik, Mary Anne Miller and Julia Mandala
Cover design by Sharon Vivian

ALL RIGHTS RESERVED. No part of this book may be reproduced or transmitted in any form by any means, electronic or mechanical, including photocopying and recording, or by any information storage and retrieval system, except as may be expressly permitted in writing from the publisher. Requests for permission or bulk orders should be addressed to Stupid Gravity Press, LLC, Attn: Rights and Permissions Department, P.O. Box 293413, Lewisville, TX 75029-3413 or StupidGravityPress@pobox.com.

Disclaimer: The publisher and author make no representation or warranties with respect to accuracy or completeness of the contents of this book and specifically disclaim all warranties, including without limitation warranties of fitness for a particular purpose. No warranty may be created or extended by sales or promotional materials. This work is sold with the understanding that the publisher is not engaged in rendering legal, veterinary, behavioral or other professional services. Neither the publisher nor the author shall be liable for damages arising heretofore. Readers should be aware that internet websites listed in this work may have changed or disappeared between the time the work was written and when it was read.

Printed in the United States of America
Paperback ISBN 978-1-946086-08-2
Hard cover ISBN 978-1-946086-09-9
eBook ISBN 978-1-946086-07-5

DEDICATION

To everyone who has dismissed that shadow out of the corner of their eye or felt an invisible cat jump on the bed. You're not crazy. You're blessed.

To Carole Nelson Douglas, your mentorship changed my life.

To Ruth McClure, I wish you and Pyewacket could tell me about your new adventure

To Weems, for his patience and support, and for always being there for me.

And to Nixie, feel free to visit anytime.

FOREWORD

Carole Nelson Douglas, my mentor, dear friend, and cat writer extraordinaire, had offered to write the foreword for *Ghost Cats 2*. For twenty-seven years, she mentored me. She advised me. She critiqued my work. In the twitch of a whisker, she was gone.

Carole started her career in journalism during the days of smoky, testosterone-filled newsrooms, when misogynistic editors believed women shouldn't cover hard news. She had to work twice as hard for twice as long, and the quality of her work had to far surpass that of her male counterparts. She was a trailblazer and a role model for women in journalism and publishing today.

Eventually she transferred her talents and skills to fiction, creating the Irene (she always pronounced it Ī-rēn-ē) Adler series tied to the Sherlock Holmes genre, and finally the Midnight Louie mystery series about a cat detective who talked to his readers and occasionally dogs, but never to the humans around him. Her first Midnight Louie book came out in 1992. The twenty-five-book series ran for the rest of her life. She wrote these always-catchy and original cozies at an average of one per year. At the time of her passing in October 2021, she had written an astounding sixty-four novels.

I met her by happenstance in 1994 at Galaxy Fair, a Dallas science fiction convention; she was classy, beautiful, and always dressed to the nines. *Cat on a Blue Monday*, her third Midnight Louie book, had just been released. She was at the con promoting it.

At the time, I was a reporter for a small-town newspaper covering local politics and events. My second article about cats had just appeared in *Cat Fancy* magazine.

She was so excited when I told her about my two cat articles that she immediately offered to sponsor me as a member of the Cat Writers' Association. That was the beginning of a new life and career for me.

From that moment, she was there to guide me, answer my questions, and encourage me. She felt strongly about supporting other writers, but she was passionate about elevating women in the craft.

No matter how many of my articles and books were published, I always worried I was doing something wrong. And Carole was always there with a useful tidbit or comforting word.

Then, in October 2021, the world lost that sparkling jewel who was Carole.

As I worked on the finishing touches of this book, I wanted to call and ask her opinion about this aspect or that detail. What about the book cover? For the first time, I have to make all these decisions without her input. Carole was a great teacher. And, hopefully, I can put all her lessons to good use.

I find comfort knowing she is back together with her own black cat, Midnight Louie, who left her many years ago.

So as you read this Foreword, know that Carole Nelson Douglas would have written something brilliant and witty.

I miss you so much, Beautiful Lady.

ACKNOWLEDGMENTS

The most beautiful experience we can have is the mysterious.
—Albert Einstein

Very few tasks of significance are accomplished by one person in a vacuum. An airline pilot has copilots and flight attendants, gate agents, and customer service reps. Then there are those behind-the-scenes contributors you never see: mechanics, ground crew, baggage handlers, food and beverage preparers, air traffic controllers, and meteorologists. Support may go back decades to the pilot's first flight instructor.

Books work the same way. The author's name may appear on the cover, but an asterisk should appear after the name to acknowledge a whole army of people who have contributed to the project. Some contributions are more visible than others.

Of course, I'm so grateful to all of you who had the courage and generosity to share your stories with me. Thank you for allowing me a peek into those intimate moments between you and your beloved kitties. Obviously, I couldn't have written this book without you.

I am also deeply grateful to Beth Adelman, my copy editor, who fine-tuned my manuscript and made me look good (as always), and to my proofreaders Marci Kladnik and Mary Anne Miller and fellow Redhead Julia Mandala, who tidied everything up. And then there are my artists, Stephanie Piro, whose illustrations made my readers smile, and Sharon Vivian, who created the drop-dead gorgeous cover I envisioned.

A special thank you to:

Carole Nelson Douglas, for being such a good friend and selfless mentor throughout my writing career. Over the past twenty-seven years, you have been a sympathetic guide, always being available with helpful advice and critiques. As I write this, I feel the need to reach for the phone and talk to you. I miss you so much.

Carol Oliver, for not only sharing her story, but for her fabulous artwork and for helping get the word out when I needed new ghost stories.

Bev Freed, thank you for the hours you spent helping me with the crazy formatting issues. Hope it looks good.

A special thanks to Julia Mandala, Arden Moore, Peggy Dee, Ruth McClure, Liz Lummus, Debbie Waller, and Marjorie Royal, who were there when I needed to brainstorm.

Martha Schipul and Sonja, my two favorite writing teachers, thank you for recognizing my spark and encouraging me.

Every day I thank God for my wonderful husband and soul mate, Weems Hutto. Your eternal patience, continual advocacy, and technical support made this book, as well as all my other books, possible.

I also want to thank Jeffy, ChanChan, George, Emily, and all my other rescued cats for keeping me company and not deleting the entire book again. (When it's time to bring another pet into your home, please adopt a homeless cat or dog. Rescued animals rock!)

And finally, I want to thank you, my readers, without whom there would be no point in writing this book. I hope you find comfort and hope within its pages.

CONTENTS

INTRODUCTION xvii

CHAPTER 1: GUARDIAN ANGELS 1

    Cat on the Wall 4

    Fats and Tripod 6

    Loki, God of Mischief 10

    The Guardian Angel with the Yellow Eyes 13

    Here Comes Trouble 16

CHAPTER 2: FELINE HARBINGERS 21

    Xena: Warrior Kitty 23

    Ghost Cat with a Light Touch 26

    Kipling's Cat 32

    Bright as Moonshine 35

    The Incorporeal Couch Potato 38

    Neera 41

CHAPTER 3: FAMILY REUNIONS 45

    The Paper Pusher 46

    Azlan 49

    A Moment in Heaven 51

    Josette 53

    Smoky Bear 56

    Iris 59

    Phoebe 61

    Pumpkin 64

    Furrdy 67

    Disco Cat 70

    Larry the Cat 73

    Pavel 75

    The Feline Phantom 77

    The Spy Who Loved Me 82

    Shadow Cat 85

CHAPTER 4: MANY HAPPY RETURNS 91

    The Baby Sitter 92

    Mom, Is That You? 96

    The Ceiling Fan Gremlin 100

CHAPTER 5: NOT MY GHOST CAT 105

    Mystery Cat/Guardian Angel 106

    Ghost Cat and the Evil Shadow 109

    Spooky Little Kitty 115

    Shadow Cat 119

    Smoky's Revelation 121

 Bedtime Visitation..124

 Marshmallow...126

 The Black Cat 129

CHAPTER 6: POSSESSED POSSESSIONS 133

 In Raisa's Image 135

 Chunk's Friendly Vet Toy 136

CHAPTER 7: GHOST CAT TRAVEL GUIDE..139

 Jerome, Arizona 140

DO YOU HAVE AN ANIMAL GHOST STORY TO SHARE?........................145

ABOUT THE AUTHOR...147

INTRODUCTION

I like to dim the lights and talk about the ghosts I've known and invite other people to tell me their stories. —Jenna Wortham

You are reading this because you've either had to say goodbye to a beloved pet (or person) and you need assurance of an afterlife, or maybe you are questioning your own sanity because you've seen cat-shaped shadows. Or maybe you just like to read ghost stories. (And who doesn't?)

Anyone who has loved cats (or any pet) over many years knows the sadness of saying goodbye. Unless something unforeseen occurs, it's almost inevitable we will outlive our pets. Speaking from experience, the loss can be overwhelming.

Before Fluffy's passing, our schedule revolved around him. We had to get up early to feed the cat (or walk the dog) and scoop the box. We had to rush home to give him medicine at a specific time. Then Fluffy is gone. Suddenly our lives no longer have a center. Even if we have a loving spouse or significant other, kids, and other pets, we feel adrift and alone.

While some people believe Fluffy's essence ceases, I have always believed we will see our pets again. Until that time, you may wonder whether the pain you feel will ever ease.

My original goal in writing *Ghost Cats* and *Ghost Cats 2* was to assure people that we will be reunited with our furry companions.

After *Ghost Cats* appeared in bookstores, readers wrote me to say that before reading the book, they feared their kitties were gone forever. But stories recounting the return of others' faithful felines renewed their hope of an afterlife reunion with all our loved ones.

With human COVID deaths approaching 6.5 million worldwide, my goal has changed. My mission has expanded to provide comfort for all whose loved ones who have passed, both four- and two-legged.

The past three years have been no picnic for any of us. Over the recent thirty-six months we have endured the COVID-19 pandemic, a polar vortex, wildfires, hurricanes, and a host of other natural and human-made disasters.

We have all suffered losses over these last few years: the loss of our loved ones, of our health, income, and even the basic feeling of safety in our own homes.

During the great 2021 Texas Snow-mageddon, a pipe ruptured and flooded our lower floor. My family's lives have been disrupted for nine months. Repairs are still under way. But that pales in comparison to what others have experienced. Almost every resident of planet Earth found themselves isolated, alone during the very time we most needed human comfort. Our mental health held on by the breadth of a cat whisker.

Because of the pandemic, some of us were unable to provide our pets with even minimal veterinary care. And when it came time to say goodbye, pandemic protocols prevented us from holding our little companions during their final moments. There was no closure. Only guilt and pain.

We don't know if Fluffy was afraid. We don't know if the veterinarian spoke softly to him as he eased into that good night. Did Fluffy know we loved him, or did he feel abandoned?

While we didn't get closure, I believe we will have a joyful reunion eventually.

How can I be so sure? Because, like everyone in this book, I experienced it myself. I got my reunion with a kitten who had passed, however brief the encounter.

In those few minutes, I got the opportunity to say, "Goodbye. I love you."

Within these pages, you will read about closure, protection, and forgiveness. These fortunate people received the closure they had once been deprived of. For them, the affirmation of an afterlife and the joy of *knowing* they will be reunited with their pets took the sting out of sharing with me those difficult final days.

Ghost Cats 2 is a symbol of our survival, in this life and the next. It's a tribute to our loved ones (two- and four-legged) who wait for us to join them on the Other Side.

Visitations come in so many forms, from the sudden appearance of a particular color of whiskers to bedtime snuggles to the unsettling meow of an invisible cat to returning in a different body.

I know my *Ghost Cats* books aren't the only ones on the market. They are, however, very different from other books in the same genre.

Every story in this book is real, shared by the person who experienced the encounter or by a close loved one. Unlike other ghost encounter books, I have not fictionalized or embellished *any* part of these accounts.

I pieced together each encounter mosaic after numerous email and/or telephone interviews. The contributor read the story, after which I continued to revise the piece until they were happy with the accuracy and tone and all the details. I only included the event in the book after the person gave me an official paws-up.

Some contributors proudly wanted their names to appear in their personal account. Others shared their experiences only under the condition of anonymity. To respect the privacy of those contributors, I used pseudonyms and obscured or changed personal details and specific information about their pets—but the encounter is as described.

Sadly, I have learned that some those who provided accounts lost their lives to the coronavirus or cancer. Some passed away after tragic accidents. Sometimes family members responded with the devastating news, encouraging me to use the story and attempting to fill in the blanks.

For the sake of simplicity, I refer to all generic cats in the book as males named Fluffy. All real cats are referred by their appropriate names and genders. When discussing specific ghost cats, I use the same pronoun as the person who shared the story.

I hope as you read this book you feel encouragement and reassurance. If you got something positive from these pages, please leave an Amazon verified purchase review. You can do that by going to your purchase history "Returns and Orders." Click on the *Ghost Cats 2* purchase. You'll see a link that says, "Write a Review." Click that and write your review. When it appears, the review should be labeled as a "Verified purchase." If you didn't like it, remember my name is Jane Smith and you are reading, "Magnificent Flowers of Antarctica."

There are other unwritten chapters in this book we call Life. Death is not the end. It is a new beginning—the beginning of what, I cannot say. But it will certainly be filled with wonders and adventure.

"I don't know why but I always feel safer with my ghost cat around."

CHAPTER 1: GUARDIAN ANGELS

More than ghosts, I believe in guardian angels. —Manini Mishra

Normally when we think of protective animals, cats don't jump to the top of the list. But from the earliest days of our relationship with small felines, kitties have been revered as defenders from threats both seen and unseen. They've protected people from famine and plague in the physical sense. They became spiritual guardians as well.

In ancient times, as the Egyptians first experimented with agriculture, they had the basics down: plant the seeds, tend the fields, harvest the crops, and eat the food. No problem. They ran into trouble when it came to storing their bounty for future use. Rats invaded the granaries, decimating the grain surplus. To further complicate things, rats carried diseases and parasites, and their presence attracted venomous snakes.

Egypt's salvation came when small wild cats living in the inhospitable desert followed the rodents' scent into the cities. There, the kitties discovered all the prey they could ever want to eat. The cats quickly reduced the rodent population, which enabled the crops to feed the people year-round. With the ability to store food for later consumption, humanity could advance from hunter-gatherers to establish real communities. We can thank our kitty cats for human civilization.

The Egyptians, as well as many other cultures, viewed cats not only as effective pest controllers, but also as spiritual defenders. One of the most popular deities of ancient Egypt was the goddess Bastet, who was depicted as either a black cat or as a woman with a cat's head. She was the goddess of cats and fertility, the protector of women, the keeper of hearth and home, and the guardian against evil spirits and disease.

The public image of family felines took a dive during the Middle Ages, when cats were slaughtered en masse across Europe. Their absence allowed the rodent population to once again explode. With no way to control the pests, rats from Asia covered with disease-carrying fleas spread the bubonic plague across the continent. The Black Death killed an estimated 25 million people—almost a third of Europe's population. It lingered in European cities for centuries. Only after cats were allowed to once again thrive did the disease subside.

It's believed cats possess healing powers that help keep their owners healthier. Studies have shown that stroking any pet will help ease emotional stress and reduce the chance of cardiovascular disease, but petting a cat specifically drastically reduces the chance that a person will suffer a stroke.[1]

Scientists theorize a cat's purr (which rumbles along between 25 and 150 Hertz[2]) is the same frequency as many medical devices used to promote bone and tissue healing.

---

[1] https://www.ncbi.nlm.nih.gov/pmc/articles/PMC3317329
[2] Lyons, Leslie A. "Why do cats purr?" Scientific American. January 27, 2003. Updated April 3, 2006. Accessed July 20, 2021.
https://www.scientificamerican.com/article/why-do-cats-purr

Less dramatic are the stories that appear on the Internet about kitties alerting their humans to medical emergencies such as cancer, diabetic crises, and imminent epileptic seizures.

Hero cats have been known to wake their families when they've detected the presence of carbon monoxide and smoke from smoldering fires, allowing the people to escape. It's not unusual for cats to protect their humans from spiders and snakes, and even dangerous animals of a far superior size.

In Bakersfield, California, in 2014, a brown tabby named Tara protected her four-year-old human from a vicious dog attack. A security camera documented a retriever mix entering the yard, grabbing the toddler by the leg, and attempting to drag him off. Tara leaped on the much larger animal, bringing all her weapons to bear. She chased the attacker out of the yard, then returned to check on her kid while the dog ran away, tail between his legs. The boy's bite wound required ten stitches.

While some cats do go full-blown mama grizzly against physical threats, as Tara did, cats may also protect us from threats we cannot see. They seem to be able to discern untrustworthy people.

Are cats psychic or are they simply scenting a pheromone emitted during the act of deceit? Cats are blessed with such acute senses that they pick up on sounds, scents, vibrations, and light frequencies humans can't detect. Regardless of where their ability to see and discern originate, they have abilities we humans don't. In living form and in spirit, they can use these abilities to safeguard their chosen people.

Some people believe cats not only have the power to detect spirits, but they can cleanse negative energies from your home. It is believed when a cat senses a paranormal entity, he follows it around the house until he determines whether its intentions are benign or malevolent.

Russians believe that a cat walking through your new home before you move in offers homeowners good luck and protection from negative energy. The belief is so widespread that in a 2014 ad campaign, Sberbank, Russia's largest bank, offered new homeowners the chance to borrow a cat for two hours, allowing him to spread protection and good luck around the house. It turned out to be a very popular campaign.

And what about kitties who have left this life? As demonstrated in the following encounters, cats who have formed strong bonds with their humans in life often return from the afterlife as guardians and protectors. The fact that they no longer need a physical body doesn't change their love for their humans or their protective nature. Maybe your ghost cat is the manifestation of a guardian angel or spirit guide.

Today, thanks to medical advances, the bubonic plague can be treated with antibiotics. But our cats still protect our barns, bestow good luck, and grace us with their affection. If we're fortunate, when they have shed their corporeal fur, they may come to us a last time or two to stand guard or say goodbye.

Cat on the Wall

In his 60 years on this Earth, Charlie Hyman had never lived with a pet, and he had no desire to change the status quo. Charlie was a very quiet, stoic man who worked as a buyer for the City of Baltimore. He enjoyed his uncomplicated home. From his observations, pets were messy and a lot of trouble. He didn't see the need for an animal padding around his castle.

The status quo was turned on its head in 1967. That was the year a friend's cat was blessed with a litter of kittens. Charlie's wife, Florence, and sixteen-year-old daughter, Carol, began a campaign to adopt one of the kittens. While Charlie wasn't enthusiastic about getting a tiny furball, he went along with it.

They named their eight-week-old kitten Schlepper, a Yiddish word meaning someone who is clumsy or inept. Little Schlepper was a tiny ball of fuzz when they got her—a basic black kitten with short hair. That basic kitten grew into a sleek basic black cat, weighing ten pounds, tops.

Even though no one in the family had any experience with animals, Schlepper made it easy for them. She fit in well and didn't demand much. A typical kitten, she got into the expected kitten mischief in the family's small Baltimore apartment—climbing curtains, knocking things off tables—but she was generally well-behaved and affectionate with the whole family. In the early days she mostly hung out with Carol, but as she matured, Schlepper's allegiance gradually shifted from Carol to Charlie.

Preferring a quiet, predictable environment, Charlie didn't dislike the new family member; he just had no interest in her. Schlepper, however, was drawn to Charlie the way that, in a roomful of people, the cat will jump in the lap of the person who least likes cats.

After dinner, Charlie traditionally settled into his favorite lounge chair with the newspaper or the latest issue of *Newsweek*. As he scribbled words in the blocks of his crossword puzzle, Schlepper shimmied her way into a small space between Charlie and the chair's arm. Defiant, she refused to move. At first, he absently stroked her fur as he filled in the six-letter word for cat. Charlie realized he *liked* having a cat. He enjoyed her sitting with him. Before long, Carol found him playing with Schlepper, teasing her with his wiggling fingers. Who knew a cat could make him so happy!

Late some evenings, Florence caught normally reserved Charlie in the middle of the floor on all fours, playing chase with Schlepper. Not only did that little black kitty turn into Charlie's personal cat, the pair became best friends. Charlie turned into an unapologetic fan of his feline friend.

Eventually, Carol moved away to live on her own. Schlepper stayed behind with Charlie and Florence.

As happens when cats age, Schlepper gradually slowed down. She developed kidney disease and stopped eating. Toward the end, she couldn't make it to the litter box. Then one day, after her sixteenth birthday, Charlie and Florence knew it was time to say goodbye. Florence called the vet to arrange that final house call. They were broken-hearted.

A year later, at the age of seventy-five, Charlie suffered a massive stroke that robbed him of his ability to walk and talk and the use of his right arm—skills the doctors said he would never get back. He spent four months in the hospital. Piling on more bad news, the medical specialists didn't believe he was he a good candidate for rehabilitation. Instead, they recommended long-term care. His family ignored the doctors and insisted he go to rehab.

Florence and Carol spent the entire first day with Charlie at the rehab center, where he had a ground-floor room. That evening, as the women pulled out of their parking spot, Carol glanced back at Charlie's window. On the short wall that encircled the center sat a black cat, eyes lock on Charlie's window. The cat looked identical to Schlepper—the same size, same shape. She didn't notice Florence or Carol, or at least, she didn't bother to look at them. Instead, the cat stared unwaveringly into Charlie's room.

Carol said to Florence, "Look at the fence."

Mom and daughter turned to each other. This was no ordinary cat. The women knew it was Charlie's little friend looking out for her human.

"That's Schlepper," Florence said. "She's watching over him."

As they drove away, Schlepper remained unmoving on the wall. As the rehab center shrunk to a tiny dot in the rearview mirror, both mother and daughter felt happy. With Schlepper watching over Charlie, they somehow knew the doctors' predictions about Charlie's recovery were wrong. Schlepper checking in on Charlie was like him having a guardian angel.

Carol believes his feline friend must have shared some sort of magic, because the next day Charlie was propelling himself around in a wheelchair. While he hasn't fully recovered from his stroke, his progress far exceeded his doctors' expectations. Although he's never regained the use of his right arm, he eventually progressed enough to go home. He can walk with the aid of a brace and a special cane, and he even regained some of his speech.

Neither Carol nor Florence ever told Charlie about the cat outside his window. Knowing Charlie, he'd just say they were nuts.

"We never saw her again," Carol said. "But we knew it was her, and she was watching over my father. After her visit, he did better in rehab than anyone had expected."

That couldn't be an accident.

*****

Schlepper was Carol Hyman's starter cat. Since then, she has adopted many cats, fostered even more, and transported hundreds to rescue. She and her husband live in downtown Baltimore with Sophie, Winston, and Argyle—three rescue kitties. To get her dog fix, she volunteers at Barcs, Baltimore's municipal shelter.

Fats and Tripod

Carol Rowland Oliver and her husband, Frank, live in a hundred-year-old home on historic Swiss Avenue in Dallas. The Victorian-style home had belonged to Frank's late wife. Cherry, his late bride of almost thirty years, took her first and last breaths in the house; she was born in the master bedroom and in 2009 she died on the sofa bed in the living room from breast cancer. When Cherry passed, she left Frank with the home and her two cat siblings, Tripod, a longhaired tuxedo, and Fats, a Siamese mix.

Built in 1920, the home was traditional in every way: hardwood flooring complemented by an elegant wooden staircase that spanned from the ground floor to the second story. Like most flooring of the time, every footstep taken up the stairs creaked throughout the lower floor.

Eventually Frank began dating. One girlfriend wanted him to get rid of both the house and the cats. Needless to say, she didn't last long.

Five years after Cherry passed, Frank met Carol, and soon they became a couple. While they were dating, he often joked about how Cherry reacted when he changed something in the house or whenever he threw away an item that belonged to her. Carol dismissed his comments.

A year later, Carol and her Birman-mix, Sophie, moved in with Frank, his cats, and (even though she didn't know it at the time) Cherry. Like many old houses, Carol could feel a presence, but she didn't think much about it. Carol soon learned Frank wasn't kidding about his late wife, though. Carol heard squeaks and creaks coming from the stairwell, but wrote it off to the house settling or a show on the television. She didn't realize there really was a ghost until she was alone in the house and she heard human footsteps on the stairs. Different footwear makes different sounds on wood planks, Carol observed, and these footfalls sounded like someone climbing the steps wearing athletic shoes—Cherry's footwear of choice. That night, Carol watched the staircase as it made squeaking noises that moved progressively higher along the steps. Beside Carol, Tripod and Fats sat on the floor, staring up at the staircase. They heard it too. Carol said the cats knew the footsteps belonged to their mama.

From then on, whenever Carol heard the footfalls on the stairs, she shrugged it off. After all, it was Cherry's house. "I never had issues with her," Carol said.

Early on she spoke to Cherry. "I hope you don't mind me being here. I promise not to hurt him."

Cherry had been a collector of Hallmark and Disney memorabilia; whenever either Frank or Carol moved parts of the massive collection, the stairwell footsteps grew louder and more frequent. Just as Frank had said, Cherry didn't like people messing with her belongings.

Carol always loved cats, so it was natural after she moved in that she fell in love with Cherry's kitties. While Fats had an appropriately descriptive name, Tripod was a misnomer. She had injured her leg as a tiny kitten, but it eventually healed. By the time Carol joined the family, Tripod had four perfectly functioning limbs. Physical issues aside, the cats were not at all interested in snuggling with a stranger. Carol spent the next few months bonding with them. She sat at the kitchen table offering them treats, something they'd never experienced before. Within four months, she taught Fats, a very food-motivated cat, to do high-fives on cue. It took another couple of months for them to fully warm up and enthusiastically crawl into her arms.

When Frank was single, the two cats slept at the foot of his bed. After Carol's accelerated bonding classes, they took turns sleeping in her arms, while Sophie slept next to her head on the pillow. When Fats wasn't snuggling with Carol, she slept against Frank's legs.

Over a long period of time, Tripod developed multiple health issues, including chronic diarrhea. Vets could never determine the source of the problem. Then one day, Tripod's health took a downward turn. Within three days, the fourteen-year-old cat passed. Two weeks later her sister, Fats, went to sleep never to wake up again.

A week after Fats' passing, Carol and Frank were relaxing in bed when they both felt a cat jump on the bed. The weight of a cat settled on the back of Carol's knees. The only living cat in the house was Sophie, and she was already curled up on Carol's pillow.

Ghost cats joining them in bed became a fairly regular event. Even though she couldn't see them, Carol could tell the difference between the two cats. The one tromping across her body was Tripod. The heavy one who laid on her had to be Fats. Without thinking, Frank would reach to his feet to pet the weight against his legs. He felt no fur, and whenever he attempted to touch it, the pressure vanished.

Within a few weeks of the ghost kitties' appearances, Carol got two kittens: Boo, pedigreed Turkish Angora, and Dot, a white kitten with tabby spots. Carol rescued them from a woman who planned to take them to the pound. Soon after, Carol was working in the kitchen. Nearby, Boo and Dot slept soundly in their bed in the window. All of a sudden, Carol heard the unmistakable sound of cats bumping around and racing up and down the stairs. When she investigated, the stairs were vacant. Once again she heard the unmistakable sounds of playing cats bounding up and down the steps, yet every time she checked, the stairwell was empty. It had to be Cherry's old kitties stopping by for a game of chase.

Cherry was a regular visitor, but had never interacted with Carol directly, except once. Two years after she moved in, Carol was awakened in the middle of the night by a woman's voice calling from the stairs, "Carol, Carol, Carol. Help me!" Carol jumped out of bed and dashed to the staircase. She found nobody there. A couple of days later, Frank was diagnosed with very early-stage throat cancer.

"I'm convinced she was asking me to help him," Carol said. "After all, she had died of cancer." Three months after Frank received the diagnosis, he saw a woman in the backyard by the gazebo facing away from him. He couldn't tell who she was, but Carol knew it was Cherry looking out for him.

During his three months of cancer treatments, Frank felt Fats' weight on his legs much more frequently. Carol said the two cats were taking care of Frank during his illness. Fortunately, Frank's cancer was caught at such an early stage that he made a full recovery.

The couple still feels the spirit cats jump on the bed; sometimes it's Fats; at other times it's Tripod. They appear more frequently when either Carol or Frank feel stressed.

In addition to Cherry's footsteps, Carol still hears the feline ruckus on the stairs a couple of times a month. All of their current cats hear it too. The fully embodied kitties all stop and stare at the stairs at the same time as Carol and Frank. It's not unusual for Carol to catch Boo and Dot playing with invisible feline playmates. They swat at the empty air, chasing invisible bugs or playmates who can't be seen with the naked eye. The games with the ghost cats happen all around the property: in the backyard, on the stairs, and all over the living room floor. Sometimes they are obviously chasing the shadows of the squirrels in the trees. The rest of the time, Carol can't tell what they're playing with.

"From the moment you get your cats, they are guardian angels," Carol said. "That doesn't stop because they die. They look out for you and see what you can't. They can sense you're sick even before you know you are. They didn't want to leave us."

*****

Carol Rowland Oliver is the human translator, illustrator and photographer for feline author and celebrity, Boo the Deaf Kitty. She and Boo coauthor the Feline Park Inspector children's book series.

Loki, God of Mischief

Tracy Big Pond has a long history with cats, dating back to her childhood. She loves kitties so much that, despite dealing with several health challenges, including fibromyalgia, in 1999 she began raising and showing pedigreed Turkish Vans.

The breed, originated from the Van Lake region in Turkey next to Mt. Ararat where several versions of legends assert that Turkish Vans are the cats who sailed aboard Noah's ark. They were named for their unique Van coat pattern that features color markings on the head and tail with some body spots against a snow-white background.

Tracy's Loki was a Turkish Van on steroids, figuratively speaking, weighing in at around thirty pounds. He had the build of a Mack truck with perfect black markings against a cashmere white coat.

One trait of the Turkish Van breed is their fascination with water. In the wild, they are known to swim in the saline Van Lake. Loki, too, loved water activities. He especially enjoyed fishing. To satisfy her Vans' fascination with water, Tracy put feeder fish in a shallow dish on the floor for the cats to catch. While they love water, not all Vans are natural anglers. A couple of her cats couldn't catch a fish even if they were starving. Ever the caring big brother, Loki always made sure all the kitties got a fish. After they had tried unsuccessfully for a bit Loki helped his companions by flipping a fish or two over to them.

Whenever the communal food or water bowls needed to be topped off, he stared at Tracy until she bent to his will. He made the same appeal when another kitty left a particularly stinky mess behind in one of the litter boxes. He wanted it cleaned—immediately.

At cat shows, when Tracy took Loki to the show ring, he usually rode draped over her left shoulder with his tail and back legs hanging down her front, all the while purring in her ear. It was show time!

He was a charmer, especially in the eyes of the cat show judges. On the judging stands, he played up to the judges, flirted with the crowd, and strutted his stuff for anyone with a camera.

He may have been a superstar in the show ring, but at night he was Tracy's bedtime buddy. Every night of their ten years together, he slept on Tracy's pillow. He started out near the edge of the pillow. Slowly, as the night progressed, he scooched closer and closer to her head until he ended up in the crook of her neck. By morning, Tracy's head was pinned against her opposite shoulder.

When Tracy realized Loki's larger-than-life personality could help people experiencing emotional turmoil and loneliness, she began training him to work as a therapy cat, focusing on senior citizens and children in elementary school special education classes. (Looking back, he would have been perfect for victims of PTSD, but at the time, that condition wasn't widely recognized in her area.)

Then, one night after Loki's tenth birthday, Tracy returned home to find only eight of her nine cats greeting her at the door. Uncharacteristically, they all acted skittish. Bella, one of the females, kept pacing back and forth in the hall. After a nose count, Tracy realized Loki wasn't with the group. She called his name, but Loki didn't respond. Finally, a soft mew answered her. She followed Bella and found him; his back legs weren't working. She immediately took him to the vet.

The vet said he'd had a stroke or possibly a blood clot. Loki's condition was painful; treatment would be brutal, expensive, and not likely to be successful. Even if he endured the treatment, it would leave him with a short, poor quality of life.

Loki's illness couldn't have happened at a worse time. Tracy was enduring her own health crisis. She had just been diagnosed with fibromyalgia and was suffering through excruciating flare-ups. At the time, her doctors had failed to regulate her medication properly. She was barely able to care for herself, much less provide intensive care for her kitty companion.

Tracy made the painful decision to end Loki's suffering. "I was thinking of his quality of life," she said. "I didn't know how I could help him get better with everything I had going. I was barely taking care of me. And that's the part that hurt. Intellectually, I knew there wasn't anything I could have done for him—not with the veterinary care available at the time."

She brought Loki home one last time. With all his humans and beloved kitty companions surrounding him, a mobile vet released him. He died in Tracy's arms. "I felt him when left his body," she said.

She felt so guilty. After everything Loki had done for her, all the painful times he'd seen her through, the comfort she had received from his snuggles and his purrs, she couldn't help him.

He was cremated and his ashes placed in a little cedar box with a plaque engraved displaying his name, show titles, and the dates he came into and left this world.

Tracy didn't handle the sudden loss well. She sunk into a deep depression. She had to take most of her cats to live with her ex-husband. Then she went to stay with her mom.

That night, when Tracy laid her head down, it seemed so wrong to have the pillow to herself. She missed Loki hogging the pillow; she even missed her achy neck. She dozed off to sleep. Before long, she awoke to find, just as he had done every night of his life, Loki had settled on the edge of the pillow. Even though he no longer had physical substance, he still managed to gradually force her head over. The next morning, she woke up, her neck throbbing as it had every morning of Loki's corporeal life. That was only the first of many Loki-inspired neck aches to come. Even today he continues to join her on her pillow.

In the beginning, he slept with her almost every night. The visits then dwindled to two or three times a week, or whenever she needed him—any time she felt down.

Loki mostly visits Tracy as she's going to sleep. Sometimes when she's walking, he drapes himself over her shoulder. He's also joined her during the day on chairs, sofas, in the car, and sometimes other places when she needs him. He always comes when she needs him most—when she's particularly stressed or in pain. As in life, when Tracy feels stressed, he purrs loudly in her ear, which never fails to calm her down.

If Loki comes to Tracy while she meditates, she can sometimes move her hand and feel him—sometimes when she's not thinking about him. If she consciously tries to touch him, nothing is there and his presence vanishes.

She believes part of the reason he visits so often is to let her know he understood why she had to euthanize him. Even with his forgiveness, she still feels guilty.

"He makes sure the cats who are still here take their duties seriously. I also think he feels the other cats can do almost as good a job of taking care of me as he could. Almost."

Since his passing in November 2009, Tracy and her son have moved half a dozen times. Through all her moves and all the belongings that have been lost or packed away, never to be seen again, she keeps Loki's ashes safe. They sit in a hallowed place in her bedroom on her bookcase.

"My books are my best possessions. My cats are my best friends," she said.

*****

Tracy Big Pond had her first book published in the third grade when several of her creative writing projects were assembled for her school's library. Since then, she has had several poems published.

The Guardian Angel with the Yellow Eyes

Sebbe, a purebred blue Persian whose real name was Sebastian, always looked out for his little human, even when she was just a wrinkly hairless kitten-baby. When Nicki Olson was just a few weeks old, nine-year-old Sebbe wanted to sleep with her. But weighing in at several pounds more than his newborn tiny person, on one occasion the overenthusiastic protector nearly suffocated her. So, sleepovers stopped until Nicki was a little sturdier. Finally, when Sebbe's kid was five years, Mom and Dad allowed him to nap next to his miniature person.

At night, he jumped on the bed, sniffed Nicki's face, then walked to the bottom left corner of her bed to settle in and sleep. Sometimes he curled up next to her chest. Happy to be with Nicki, he purred. He had a very recognizable purr. At first, he rumbled rapidly in and out as he breathed. Later, after settling down on the bed, the purr changed from pulsing to a constant vibration. He was never much of a conversationalist. He seldom meowed, but when he did, it too was distinctive.

Nicki always loved his bright yellow eyes, comparing them to twin suns. As a kid, she loved to brush his luxurious silver-gray fur.

Sebbe tolerated the dreaded doll clothes phase of Nicki's development. Despite a host of indignities foisted on him by his little girl, he adored her. He was her confidante, and he helped her through the angst every kid endures.

Sebbe turned nineteen around the time Nicki completed her first decade on Earth. For an almost two-decade-old kitty, Sebbe had few health problems. However, one evening Nicki and the family came home from Christmas shopping to find Sebbe unresponsive. He was leaving this life. That was the Christmas the Olson family didn't bother to celebrate. Nicki missed her feline friend terribly.

A few months later, when Nicki got up in the middle of the night to go to the bathroom, she watched a pair of huge, glowing yellow eyes levitate across the living room and hover a foot above the floor. Unable to move or scream, she simply stared helplessly. The eyes blinked slowly at her, and then vanished—like special effects in a horror movie. That night she couldn't fall sleep for fear the eyes would return.

At first, the experience terrified her: disembodied eyes flying toward her in the middle of the night. A day or two later, though, Nicki realized that the presence wasn't malevolent. Nothing bad had happened to her when she saw the eyes. They didn't chase her; they didn't hurt her. Realizing this, her fear eased. As time passed, Nicki could think about her vision more objectively. There was something familiar about those eyes. They were ginormous. Then she began reminiscing about her old kitty. Those huge floating eyes were the same size and shape as Sebbe's eyes. The yellow eyes were more vivid than any other cat's. Suddenly Nicki had an epiphany. The eyes belonged to her best friend, Sebbe! Her protector was still with her.

When Nicki had stood eye-to-eye with Sebbe that night, her mind told her to run, scream, or do something, but her ten-year-old body refused to move. Looking back, she's happy she didn't interrupt that magic moment. Sebbe had died so suddenly, she didn't have a chance to say all the things she wanted to say: *Goodbye. I'll miss you. I love you.* Since that nighttime encounter, Nicki has learned that a slow blink is a sign of feline affection—a kitty kiss. Sebbe came back to tell her goodbye. Or so she thought.

One night not long after her realization, she was in bed with her head on the pillow when she felt the energy in her bedroom suddenly change. There was a lightness in the air; a benevolent presence appeared in her bedroom. Then something jumped on the bed. It moved toward her head. She felt the distinctive sensation of a cat sniffing her face. Sebbe! Spirit Sebbe snuggled next to her chest. Then she heard the comforting sound she had heard all her life, a faint in and out purr transforming to the soft and constant rhythm like a spring rain. She felt around but found no kitty. It had to be Sebbe; the Olsons didn't have another cat at the time.

Sebbe became a frequent nighttime guest. Whenever he arrived, she could always tell; the energy in the room transformed and felt lighter. She usually felt the sensation of a cat jumping on the bed, padding across the blanket, and then lying down by her feet.

Sometimes she felt him walking around on the bed looking for his spot, as if he was trying to get comfortable before going to sleep.

Some nights, specter Sebbe snuggled closer to her face and purred. Whenever she tried to concentrate on the purr, it grew so faint she couldn't hear it, but whenever she relaxed and tried to sleep, the purr grew louder. When Nicki reached down to pet the invisible cat, nothing was there. She felt only a depression in the mattress. Whenever she peeked, she never actually saw the indentation, but she felt the pressure against her body until she fell asleep.

At first, Sebbe appeared almost nightly. As the years passed, his physical visits grew fewer and farther apart.

Over the next few years, Nicki saw other apparitions—the only difference being these seemed more human and less feline. At first, they disturbed her. Eventually, she realized the specters really didn't mean to scare her or cause her harm; they merely existed.

As a fourteen-year-old, Nicki began to feel the presence of a new energy, something dark. She often felt a heavy sensation when she went into her closet. Sometimes out of the corner of her eye, she caught a shadow in the mirror. Its presence unsettled her. The atmosphere became much more ominous after she invited a friend for a sleepover. Earlier, Nicki had confided in her friend about the presence. Unbeknownst to Nicki, the girl had brought a Ouija board. Nicki left the room to get some snacks. When she returned, she found her friend communicating with the entity. Nicki took the board away and sent the girl home. But it was too late. The connection was made. Whatever it was, the pitch-black entity had never been human.

For years, the dark spirit hung around her all the time. It began entering her dreams.

Even after the appearance of the sinister presence, Sebbe dropped by once or twice a week, although not as frequently as when she was little. The appearances slowly faded when she was a late teen and young adult to every couple of months.

Soon after she turned twenty, Nicki gave birth to her son, Raymond. However, shortly after his birth she felt the dark entity lingering around him. When Raymond was just a couple of weeks old, Nicki was awakened by Sebbe's distinctive meow. She shot straight up in bed and instinctively looked at Raymond's crib. Leaning over the newborn was the shadowy figure.

Mama bear Nicki did what she needed to protect her baby. "I'm not sure what I did, but I filled the room with mother's love and for a moment, everything went pink." The dark spirit dissolved. That was the last time it ever came around. Just as Sebbe had fiercely protected Nicki as a baby, he also protected Raymond. Nicki knows Sebbe woke her to warn her about the entity's threat to his new little human.

After Nicki's new cat, Mystique, and her litter of kittens entered Nicki and Raymond's life, Sebbe stopped visiting as regularly. However, even today he makes an appearance once or twice a year.

While he no longer shares her bed, he frequents her dreams, especially when she's stressed about something.

*****

Nicki Olson is a loving mother to cats, dogs, and a little boy. She has always been intrigued by the paranormal side of the world.

Here Comes Trouble

Growing up, Kyliejean Pearn, from New South Wales, Australia, seldom stayed in one city for long. Her father served in the Royal Australian Navy and, as with any military family, they moved all over the country.

Just six months before Kyliejean was born, her Mum rescued Trouble, a tiny stray kitten. By the time Kyliejean came into the world, Trouble had grown into a fearless six-month-old pure black cat with jade eyes.

Through the years, family members disagreed on who Trouble

really belonged to. Kyliejean's sister believed Trouble was her cat, but Kyliejean knew he was bonded to her. After all, Sis left home when Trouble was four years old, and much younger Kyliejean stayed with him until she turned eighteen.

Whenever the family arrived at a new military base, Kyliejean's Mum always rubbed butter on his paws because an old wives tale claimed it helped cats find their way back to their new homes. More likely, he found his way home by following the scent of salmon that Mum left on the porch for him.

If Trouble had a job title, it would have been "ultimate hunter." He took down lizards and spiders and left them at the front door. He fought whatever unfortunate creatures crossed his path.

Australia is home to some of the deadliest life forms on the planet. Trouble had no qualms about challenging any of them. One of the world's deadliest spiders, the hairy black funnel web spider, which can grow as large as an adult human's palm, is known for its aggression, enormous fangs and lethal bite. They burrow into the ground and weave a funnel-shaped web that conveniently delivers prey directly into their den. The venom of some species can kill an adult human in fifteen minutes.

Kyliejean recalls that countless funnel spider webs covered their yard. Obviously, a cat as territorial as Trouble had to put a stop to that. Once a week for the two years they lived in that house on Lane Cove in Sydney, he left a dead spider on the porch of the home.

When one particular arachnid set up shop in Trouble's yard, he didn't hesitate to take it out. One afternoon the family returned home to find Trouble in the middle of a funnel web engaged in a life and death battle with a spider. Kyliejean never saw him miss his mark. Patient and calculating, Trouble watched and waited for his adversary to make a mistake. Kyliejean never knew whether Trouble killed his arachnid foe that day, but the spider's fangs made contact at least a couple of times.

Despite the confirmed bites, Trouble suffered no ill effects. His vet theorized that after so many encounters with the spiders, he had built up immunity to the venom.

Kyliejean's dad suffered from bipolar disorder, so the entire family was at the mercy of his mood swings. Kyliejean, an introvert, often felt overwhelmed by her father's temper and the outside world. Trouble often sat on Kyliejean's lap, and when Mum wasn't looking, he snuck into Kyliejean's room and dropped down next to her in bed. Trouble was Kyliejean's protector and comforter. He anchored her. His purr calmed her, and his cheekiness made her smile.

Kyliejean called him her Little Black Lion, but after she saw the movie *The Jungle Book*, he became her Little Panther. He once chased a German Shepherd down the road because he thought the dog was menacing her. The shepherd's nose bore scars from Trouble's claws until the day he died.

Trouble was fearless, strong, and free, yet he was so gentle and loving with Kyliejean. When she was six, she broke her arm. Trouble, the comforter, sat beside her every minute until her cast came off twelve weeks later. He didn't hunt. He only left the house for bathroom breaks, then he rushed back to her side.

Eventually, Kyliejean grew up, and at age eighteen, she got married and moved away. Not long after, Trouble's health began to decline. He suddenly lost a lot of weight; the vet suspected cancer. Unfortunately, Kyliejean couldn't be with Trouble when he was put to sleep. Mum believed since he didn't need to protect his young human any longer, he could leave the world in peace. That would prove to be untrue.

Kyliejean's marriage wasn't what she hoped it would be. After several years, she left her abusive husband and flew across the country to live with her parents again. It felt odd to walk into that familiar home. Everything looked the same, but her faithful black cat wasn't waiting for her at the door. Her parents converted the garage into an apartment until Kyliejean could get back on her feet.

Her life was in a state of flux. She waited in limbo for the court to make a decision in her child custody case. Her ex refused to let her take of so many of her personal possessions, including the one she wanted more than anything: the only existing photo of her departed little Troublemaker. She remembered it so well. Trouble had been sleeping on a white plastic chair on the family's screened porch. He'd been lying upon an old, 1980s-style sweater of Kylie's. The block pattern with pastel purple, blue, yellow, and green contrasted starkly against his black fur. Sleepy-eyed, he was in the process of waking up when the photo was taken.

Even Mum and Dad didn't have any surviving pictures; it was her last tangible piece of Trouble. She'd have given almost anything to have that photo back.

At night, Kyliejean while sitting on the back step where Trouble had left his trophies, found herself crying under the stars. Unlike moments in the past when she shed tears, Trouble wasn't there to snuggle next to her, reminding her that everything would work out.

One afternoon, her mother had been harping about the "trouble" Kyliejean had brought upon herself, and Kyliejean responded, "I wish Trouble was here and not the stuff you're nagging me about!"

Starting that night, little things began to happen. Dead spiders and lizards appeared in her doorway. At first, she thought it was the result of some neighborhood animal. She just ignored the offerings. But after two weeks of nightly presents, she began hearing scratching at the door around two in the morning. The first time, it scared the living beejeebers out of her. Her new partner told her to "go back to sleep. It was just a possum."

The following night, when she was alone, the noise happened again. Rattled, she told herself it was just one of the local cats. Turning over in her bed, she chose to ignore it.

The two a.m. scratching went on for five days. Finally, sleep-deprived Kyliejean got pissed off and opened up the door to . . . nothing. No possum, no cat. But she felt something cat-like brush past her legs. Dismissing everything, she returned to bed. Unlike the troubled nights of past months, she fell into a comfortable, restful sleep. The next morning, she awoke to the feeling of something warm against her back. The warmth faded as she cleared the cobwebs from her mind.

The following night, the scratching started up again. She opened the door once more and said, "Whoever this is, at least do this just before I fall asleep, please?" Once again, as she woke up in the morning she felt the warm pressure against her back and vibrations running down her spine from a cat's thunderous purr.

The next evening, she turned in around eleven. A few minutes later, she heard a cat crying and scratching at the door. Her heart leapt. This was no random cat; it was Trouble. As he always had, her kitty comforter knew when she was upset.

She opened the door and said, "Come on in, Troubs. I feel so lonely and hurt and I don't know what to do. Can you sleep with me so I don't get bad dreams, just like when I was little?"

She didn't hear anything, but she felt him twine around her legs. Returning to bed, she distinctly felt Trouble jump on the bed and settle next to her back, his favorite position.

For the next three years, the pattern continued almost nightly. He appeared only if she was alone and only if she had been crying.

The visits continued until she met her current husband, Ben, after which she seldom spent the night alone.

One morning after Trouble's visit, she found that one and only existing photo of her precious cat lying on her doorstep, just as he had left all his other trophies. She held the picture, lovingly touching the black cat in the image she knew so well—his back arched in a vigorous stretch, mouth open in a yawn with a little glimpse of his pink tongue sticking out, looking a little sleepy after a nap. How was it possible? She examined every detail.

This was the same photo that her ex-husband vindictively held on to at the other end of the country.

Kyliejean didn't know it at the time, but that would be her last encounter with Trouble. She believes Trouble knew she was finally happy. He wanted her to know he knew. While Trouble ceased to appear, Kyliejean felt the peace and happiness that she'd felt snuggling with her feline protector.

Years later, Kylie purchased a black cat pin that reminded her of Trouble to wear to a cat show. After she wore it, she put it away safely in her drawer. Later, when she wanted to wear the pin, it wasn't there. After a thorough search of the house, she found it in another room entirely, in a box of photos next to her treasured picture of Trouble. Now, whenever she wears that pin, she knows Trouble is with her. No matter how many cat shows she attends, the pin always seems to jump out at her, reminding her to wear it. The old adage may go, "Curiosity killed the cat," but for her own purposes, Kyliejean has changed it to, "Curiosity and the killed cat never fade."

*****

Kyliejean Pearn is a proud military wife, mother, and grandmother who teaches special education on the South Coast of New South Wales, Australia.

"I see travel in your future... looks like an upcoming trip to the vet!"

CHAPTER 2: FELINE HARBINGERS

"It always gives me a shiver when I see a cat seeing what I can't see."
—Eleanor Farjeon

Cats know things—somehow. It doesn't seem to matter whether Fluffy is still enjoying his corporeal body or has already shed his earthly fur for a more luminescent coat, they know things. And on occasion, they share a warning with us.

It's hard to explain how cats can predict or sense impending disaster. History is full of examples of cats saving themselves from deadly catastrophes both natural and human-made.

A mother cat traveling with *Titanic* crewman Joe Mulholland carried her kittens, one-by-one, off the doomed ship at the last port stop before *Titanic* hit the iceberg. The cat not only saved herself and her kittens, but also her human, who observed her exodus and left the ship right behind her.³ How could she have known?

During World War II, Faith, the church cat at St. Augustine's Church in London, saved herself and her kitten, Panda, from a German bombing raid. On September 6, 1940, Father Henry Ross, vicar of St. Augustine's, noticed Faith carrying Panda from the warm rectory down to the cold, dank basement. Father Thomas retrieved Panda and brought him back upstairs into the warmth because he didn't want the kitten getting chilled. Before long, Faith carried her kitten back downstairs. The third time she took Panda to the basement, Father Thomas let them stay. The following night, the church was leveled by German bombs. Fortunately, Father Thomas was away at the time. When he returned on September 9 to the rubble that had been his church, he began digging frantically through the still-burning ruins and calling Faith's name. Finally, from beneath the pile of stone and wood, she answered him. Both Faith and Panda survived. Somehow, she knew to take her baby underground the day *before* the bombs fell.⁴

You've probably experienced your own cats' ability to foretell the future. In a less dramatic display of feline perception, Fluffy always knows, even before the carrier appears, that he's going to the vet. As soon as you start to *think* about the veterinary appointment or are about retrieve the carrier from the closet, Fluffy makes himself invisible.

Cats often react fearfully to an oncoming thunderstorm when it is still counties away. While you're just seeing the storm on weather radar, your cat has already been cowering in his favorite hiding place for hours. Reactions to approaching storms can be explained by cats detecting a change in barometric pressure or ultra-high or low-frequency sounds emitted by the storm that are beyond the human ability to hear. Disappearing before an earthquake may be the result of an undetectable (to humans) vibration or gases released from the ground. Predicting the human's arrival could be the cat's phenomenal sense of hearing, but what about when the person returns at an arbitrary time of day or in a different car?

Do cats have a sixth sense or are they simply gifted with superpower senses? How do you explain Joe Mulholland's *Titanic* cat

---

³ Molony, Senan. *The Irish Aboard Titanic*. Wolfhound Press. Dublin. 2001.
⁴ Patrick Roberts. "Faith." Purr 'n' Fur. May 2004. http://www.purr-n-fur.org.uk/famous/faith.html. Accessed 7-28-2021.

or St. Augustine's Faith escaping events that can't be predicted or detected through the five senses?

This chapter has many examples of ghost cats predicting the impending death of a beloved human or animal companion. Other stories include cats determined to say goodbye, appearing to their person as they are walking through the veil to their next adventure.

So yes, cats know things. Sometimes, if we are paying attention, they're kind enough to give us a whisker up.

Xena: Warrior Kitty

Paul Palika had never lived around cats until he met his wife, Liz. Even then, most of their cats were bonded to Liz—at least until Xena arrived.

Xena joined the family when Liz stopped by an Oceanside, California grocery store on the way home from a dog training class with her Australian Shepherds, Dax and Riker. As she pulled into the parking space, an eight-week-old kitten dashed past her. Liz knew if she didn't do something, the kitten wouldn't survive long in that busy parking lot. Every time Liz got within a few feet, though, the feral kitten darted away. A capable strategist, the kitten hid inside shrubbery, which offered cover along with multiple escape exits.

She was an old-fashioned tabby—shorthaired brown sporting black stripes punctuated with blue eyes just turning to gold. Huddled in the parking lot, the kitten appeared adorable and fragile. Cornered, with her wild eyes, ears flat and visible teeth, she looked as fierce as a Tasmanian devil.

To catch this stray, Liz needed help, and she had the experts for the job. She brought out her dogs, ordering them to sit-stay on either side of the bush. As Liz hoped, the kitten was so focused on the dogs she didn't notice Liz inching next to her. Liz grabbed the kitten, who immediately sunk all eighteen claws into Liz's chest, where they remained imbedded until they arrived home.

Liz unpeeled the kitten from her skin, and handed her to Paul. From that moment the little feral kitty bonded to him. After all, Paul had saved her from the crazy woman who chased her around the parking lot.

Paul, a Vietnam-era Marine veteran, suffered from PTSD. Whether he knew he needed her or not, the feral kitten transformed into a powerful therapy pet. He named her Xena, after the old television series Xena: Warrior Princess. Her personality, along with her emotional strength, was so much more than should have fit into that tiny feline body.

Paul was puzzled by the feral kitten's devotion. But Xena's persistence eventually won him over. Whenever he was home, she hung out next to him. He was Xena's heart and soul. Every morning, she stood vigil in the bathroom sink while he showered. Then she followed him into the bedroom to help him dress. After he left for work each day as a safety specialist for the Department of Defense, Xena took possession of his favorite chair, protecting it until Paul returned.

As soon as Paul arrived home from work, Xena hovered within his arm's reach. She followed him from room to room. Whenever he stayed in one spot, Xena had to touch him in some manner. In bed, she slept on his chest or his back; when he sat down, she napped on the back of his chair. She purred for him, which research has shown to have healing properties. Whenever she purred, his Vietnam War-based bouts of anger or self-loathing decreased significantly.

Xena even coexisted peacefully with the Palikas' other cats and dogs. As much as she loved Paul, though, Xena rejected Liz. Despite being the one who fed her and cleaned the litter box, Liz couldn't touch her. Throughout her entire life, Xena continued to blame Liz for the trauma in parking lot.

One rainy morning in late March 2011, after Paul left for work, Xena, who was still strong and healthy, slept peacefully on his side of the bed. At 6:32, she startled awake, letting out a prolonged shriek right out of a Stephen King movie—earsplitting and heartbroken. All four dogs ran to her, but she continued to howl. Upon hearing her, Liz immediately feared the seventeen-year-old cat was sick or hurt. But after a few minutes, Xena calmed down and claimed Paul's living room chair, as usual.

While she ate breakfast, Liz watched the local news. One reporter was covering a fatal motorcycle accident that resulted in the closing of Interstate 805, one of San Diego's major freeways. Liz didn't think any more of it until a couple of hours after Xena's outburst one of Paul's coworkers called asking if he was home sick. He had never made it to work. Paul was that motorcycle rider in the news story. Xena had begun her mournful wail at the very moment Paul left his body.

"Once I'd been notified, I realized why she was crying," Liz said. "I couldn't explain it logically, but I knew. Even though I'm normally a scientific, prove-it-to-me type, I knew without a doubt that she knew when he died."

That day, Xena wandered the house, crying, searching for Paul. Uncharacteristically, Xena allowed Liz to wrap her in Paul's pillowcase. Once Xena was surrounded by her human's scent, she stopped yowling. Liz covered her with sheets from his side of the bed as family and friends flooded into the home. Paul's service dog, Archer, who fortunately hadn't gone to work with Paul that morning, joined Xena in bed for a few hours as she gradually calmed down.

She constantly looked for Paul, slept in his closet, and every once in a while, she looked into Liz's eyes and cried. "She either blamed me for his disappearance or was asking me to bring him home, or both," Liz said.

After Paul's death, Xena's distrust of Liz increased. "She became even more feral. I couldn't touch her and she'd run from me if I tried. We coexisted, both grieving."

A month after his death, Xena curled up in Paul's closet on his shirt she'd pulled from its hanger. There, enveloped by his scent, Xena went to sleep never to awake.

"She had shown no symptoms," Liz said. "If one could die of a broken heart, I truly believe Xena did—especially since she died so soon after Paul."

The next day, Liz was sitting at her desk writing at her computer. She stopped for a moment to work the kinks out of her spine. She raised her hands over her head, stretched, and then leaned forward, hands dropping to the floor. Beneath one hand Liz felt a cat nuzzling back and forth against her fingers. She felt the softness of the fur and the vibration of a cat's purr. Although she saw nothing physical, she immediately recognized the body, sturdy and strong, as Xena. Liz felt a wave of happiness. Then the sensation disappeared.

"I was startled," Liz said. "It only lasted for a few seconds—long enough for my brain to go, 'Oh!' I wasn't too shocked because I've always been open to things that can't be explained, even though I'm not sure I believed in the paranormal. Truly, I'm not sure why she stopped by. She didn't like me. I like to think that she found Paul and came back to tell me she was happy."

Xena never visited Liz again. Liz doesn't expect her to return. "She wasn't my cat; she was his, and I'm happy they found each other again."

Not long after Xena's visit, Liz began fostering kittens again. She had cared for homeless kitties when she was younger, and in Xena's memory she once again takes lost, orphaned, or endangered kittens until they are healthy enough to go to loving forever homes.

It's been eleven years since Paul and Xena passed away. Liz, along with her animal companions, have rescued and rehomed more than two hundred kittens—all because of one strong, opinionated, tremendously devoted tabby.

*****

Liz Palika is an award-winning writer and author as well as a retired dog trainer. Currently she shares her home with three English Shepherds—Bones, Hero, and Seven—as well as one cat, Kirk. The number of foster kittens in residence varies.

Ghost Cat with a Light Touch

Every adult child knows that when you visit your parents who live any distance away, your folks always ask you to let them know when you've made it home. It doesn't matter whether you're first going off to college or receiving Social Security benefits, we never get too old to reach out to our parents that we've safely arrived. For humans, that means a phone call or a text message.

Cats have to be a little more creative about their messaging. All of Becky Fredericks' cats who have crossed the Rainbow Bridge communicate with her through touch lamps.

Becky, a retired policy advisor for the U.S. Environmental Protection Agency, and her husband, Stan, moved into their home near Annapolis, Maryland, in 1990. Along with two kitties, they brought with them all the normal furnishings: beds, tables, sofas, chairs, and two sets of touch-sensitive lamps she had picked up at a department store several years earlier.

Touch lamps, which were very popular in the 1980s, turn on and off by human touch rather than using a mechanical switch. Becky loved the convenience, so she set up a matching pair of touch table lamps in their new living room and another pair on her bedside tables. After reading for a while, she could effortlessly turn off the light before drifting off to sleep.

Unlike most touch lamps that turn on and off at the slightest brush of the fingers, one of Becky's living room table lamps was a bit fussy. Once on, it took numerous intentional taps to extinguish it. Sometimes Becky had to press it as many as twenty times to turn it off. Still, she enjoyed it, so a little inconvenience wasn't a big deal. She just kept tapping until the light responded.

Because they lived in an area where lack of power translates to lack of water, the Fredericks equipped their new home with a whole-house electric generator. The new appliance certainly offered peace of mind. She wasn't going to have to worry about a power outage disrupting the home's furnace or even her nighttime reading.

In 1997, the Fredericks received the gift of a blue point Siamese kitten from a friend. They named him Chase the Blues Away. Although she had other cats who she loved dearly, Chase quickly became Becky's heart cat.

A typical Siamese, he was active and communicative. On several occasions during his kitten zoomies period, he knocked the bedside lamp off the nightstand. More than once, Becky found it dangling precariously by the cord a foot above the floor. Even after the rough handling, the rugged appliance still worked for years.

Time marched on. Before long the rambunctious kitten turned twelve. In 2010, Chase developed intestinal cancer and Becky had to say goodbye. The vet came to the house to let him leave life in his own place. Stan wasn't home, leaving Becky alone with Chase and the vet.

The Fredericks' other cats watched the procedure from a distance. To create a calm environment, Becky played a soft piano concerto on her iPod. She held Chase in her lap, stroking his head gently. She asked him to let her know he'd made it to the Other Side. Just as the vet gave him the injection, the music switched to the Beatles singing their rock classic, "Come Together."

Becky was surprised by the spontaneous music change. She looked at the other cats circling Chase from a distance. "I guess this is what we were supposed to do," she thought. "Come together, right now, over me." She said goodbye to Chase just one month shy of his thirteenth birthday.

It felt like the end of the world. Becky was distraught, miserable, inconsolable.

Within a week, Becky read a book late into the night, as she always did. At around two in the morning, the bedside touch lamp simply turned off, the room instantly became pitch dark. She expected the power generator to immediately kick on, but it didn't.

At first, she thought it was a blackout. From her bed, however, she could see that lights in other parts of the house were still on. Nothing else turned off. Becky tapped the lamp and, faithfully, it again washed the room in light.

"What's this about?" she asked herself aloud. In the first few seconds, it frightened her, but then her mind immediately went to Chase. It had to be him. Finally, she asked the lamp, "Chase, is that you?" Not surprisingly, the lamp didn't respond. She turned off the light and left the room. When she returned later, the lamp burned brightly.

Several nights later, she headed to bed and found the touch light was already illuminating the bedroom. That, too, was weird. This time, it should have been off.

All those years living in the house with the lamp, never had it turned off or on without a human touch. Since Chase's passing, it regularly switches itself on.

She thought back to the previous week. Had the light turned on and she simply hadn't noticed? It's much easier to dismiss an already-illuminated lamp than a light that suddenly turns itself off. "When the room went dark, that got my attention," she said.

From then on, any time she talked about Chase, within a couple of hours the light came on. Whenever she thought about him, if she later walked past the lamp, the bulb burned brightly.

Since the night Chase turned the light off, her cats who have crossed over delivered messages by turning the lamp on. Sometimes they just signal hello or offer Becky encouragement when she's having a hard day. Other times they let her know a cat is sick or nearing transition. Since Chase, at least five of them have used the touch lamps to announce they were leaving. Becky began noticing the light became more active for several days in a row whenever one of her cats was sick, dying, or had recently passed.

A couple of times, the lamp issued a warning. After the light came on, the Fredericks took Claire (another Siamese) to the vet. She had undiagnosed kidney disease. They began giving her frequent rounds of subcutaneous fluids. Thanks to the lamp's warning, Claire lived another six months.

After the light turned on many days in a row, they also took Becky's new heart cat, Holly (Claire's sister), to the vet. Holly was diagnosed with an autoimmune disease that ultimately led to nasal cavity cancer. With treatment, she lived another three years. As her condition deteriorated, every day Becky looked to the lamp with trepidation. And every day she let out a sigh of relief when it remained dark. At the time, Stan didn't tell her the light had indeed been on before he left for work early in the morning. As Holly's health declined, Becky finally asked Stan about the light. He said, "Oh, yeah, it was." He turned it off before he left and promptly forgot about it.

Becky believes the light is the portal. Whenever one of their older cats develops health issues, Becky and Stan monitor the light. If it comes on, they think, "Oh, no!"

"I understand it as them letting me know that someone is not well," she said. "It's like Chase is warning me."

When Stan's favorite cat, Claire, was struggling with end-stage kidney failure, Stan found the light on and said, "Turn off. You can't have her."

Stan, who was a bona fide skeptic, now accepts that it's communication from beyond the grave. He believes the kitties who have already left this earthly plane return to escort those preparing to leave.

Even their veterinarian knows what it means when Becky tells him, "The lamp turned on yesterday." When one of Becky's cats has taken a downward spiral, the vet always asks, "Is the lamp turning on yet?"

When the health of one of their kitties is failing, during their final two weeks, the light turns on every day. After the kitty passes, the light often ceases to be active. Frustrated, Becky once told the lamp, "You can at least tell me you got there okay." Later that day, it turned on.

After Holly passed, the light didn't come on. Becky reminded the lamp, "You're always supposed to call after you get there." Just like the forgetful teenager texting, "Oops, my bad," within a couple of hours it came on.

"Apparently they're really busy when they get there with the all-you-can-eat buffet and getting together with old friends," Becky said.

The light isn't just about predicting impending tragic events. It also communicates when Becky feels distressed. If it hasn't come on, she asks if everyone is okay, and within a day or two it will respond, shining brightly.

As often happens in families when adult children move away and become too preoccupied to call their parents to just say hi, sometimes Becky doesn't hear from the cats in a while. Curious, she'll ask the lamp for a sign. The light comes on to tell her, "Hi, everything is okay."

"I can ask for a sign and I get one," she said.

Becky's cats aren't the only ones who communicate through electric lights. Seven years ago, Becky's brother, Ed, died from ALS, also known as Lou Gehrig's disease. In his final hours, she raced down the highway, breaking who knows how many traffic laws to try to see him one last time. Half an hour away, she sensed Ed's presence in the car with her. Becky understood his distress, and told him, "Ed, go! If you have the chance to get out of your frozen body, take it!" A few minutes later, she received a call from a family member telling her she could slow down; he was gone. He had passed around the time she told him it was okay to let go.

The next day, at the funeral home, while making arrangements for Ed's service, Becky and Stan sat alone in a conference room waiting for the director to return with some paperwork. Suddenly, the room went dark. Becky assumed a motion sensor decided there wasn't enough movement and shut off the light. Both Becky and Stan began waving their arms to activate the overhead lights. A few moments later, the funeral director returned and caught them crazily waving their arms around. He watched for a few moments, amused, then apologized for the power failure. The entire downtown area had gone dark.

Becky and her husband looked at each other and started laughing. "Message received, Ed. Loud and clear!" Like her beloved kitties, she knew Ed was Home and he was okay. Ed, as well as the rest of the family, had known about Becky's cats and the lamp. Perhaps he liked the idea, at least that one time.

Until several years ago, all ghost kitties' communications happened through the bedside lamp. Then it stopped working, probably the result of one too many launches off the nightstand by resident kittens. The physical on/off switch still worked, but it no longer operated as a touch lamp. Becky bought a new touch mechanism, but the cats refused to communicate through it.

"I didn't want to lose the lamp because it was my connection with my cats," she said.

Chase and the crew were determined to stay in touch. She still had the two matching table lamps in the living room. After the nightstand lamp died, the cats moved their portal to one of the lamps in the other room.

"As a touch lamp it's a failure," she said. "It takes multiple touches to turn it on or off."

A bit of a skeptic herself, Becky knows people assume there was a short in the lamp's wiring or some other mechanical issue. She's gone over what other stimuli could cause the lights to spontaneously turn on: a cat walking past, an electrical short, or a power surge? These explanations might work for an occasional spontaneous turning on, but not for the years of communication they've experienced.

As recently as July, 2021 lightning struck near their home causing the other house lights to flicker on and off. The surge not only switched the ceiling fan on, but kicked it on high. The ordinary touch light switched on too. However, the living room portal lamp didn't even flicker.

After the strike, Becky happened to be looking directly at the living room portal light when it came on. Nothing touched it—not a wave of a cat tail—nada. It just came on.

"It's one thing to walk into the room and find the light on," she said. "It's another thing to watch it happen with your own eyes. It was weird. I got goosebumps, but I didn't feel a chill or a sense of electricity or the presence of a spirit."

Becky doesn't believe her cats are necessarily unusual. "Any time you lose a pet, look around," she said. "You will see a sign. There are always signs if you watch for them.

"I wish we understood death better. We cling so desperately to life, but I think we have just forgotten how beautiful the Other Side is. At least I hope I am correct about that!"

*****

Becky Fredericks was born into a cat-loving family and has never been without a cat in all of her seventy-plus years. She said her life has definitely been better for it!

Kipling's Cat

Some cats are never yours, but they have a presence. They affect you. And when they're no longer around, they leave a hole in your life.

The day after Marcia Wilson and her best friend, Laura, moved into their new apartment near Tacoma, Washington, a dainty, brown tabby cat with rich black stripes showed up at the patio screen door. She certainly did not want in, but the one- or two-year-old tabby was hungry.

The landlady thought the cat belonged to her new tenants, but she didn't. Marcia kept her own two cats strictly inside. The ladies were already at the city's legal pet limit. Most likely, as often happens in college towns, someone moved away and left the cat behind.

The tabby made it clear she had no interest in venturing inside. She tolerated the women as neighbors, allowing them to join her as she sunned herself on the warm deck. In exchange, Marcia and Laura left food for her. But the young cat wouldn't let them get anywhere near her. She ate the cat food, but only if she was satisfied the patio door was shut with the humans safely inside. If Marcia or Laura walked outside, the cat darted away.

Marcia recalls the cautious kitty as delicately aloof, a fine lady crossed with a wild child. She assumed the cat had been someone's pet once—and that once had been enough. Marcia thought of her as Kipling's Cat, because in *The Cat that Walked by Himself* Rudyard Kipling wrote, "All places were the same to him."

They dubbed her Mama Kitty that first evening when she slipped through the pool of backyard lights and rocks with two tiny shapes in her shadow: a coal-black kitten and a golden tiger tabby. Mama Kitty was the only possible choice for a name. From her reaction, she was already familiar with it; she flicked her ears whenever they called her name at mealtime.

Mama Kitty's kittens ate happily and grew up quickly. Laura located a volunteer trap-neuter-return group that helped capture the family. Mama Kitty, caught inside the trap, thrashed around and flung herself against the wire sides. She even pierced Laura's hand with a couple of well-placed canines. Laura knew it wasn't Mama

Kitty's fault; the cat was certain these large human predators were going to eat her. The kittens were also terrified of their strange surroundings. Before long, they were all altered, vaccinated and de-flea-d. Within a few days, the trauma was behind them, and the women released the cats back into the neighborhood.

Feral cats don't live nearly as long as indoor cats. Between the aggressive predators who lived nearby, speeding cars, and deadly diseases, ferals' lifespans are often half that of an indoor cat. Marcia and Laura were desperate to bring Mama Kitty inside and find her a home, but the suspicious, self-reliant young mother refused their help.

Everything was perfect at the time, but cold weather was approaching. After the air turned crisp and cold, the black kitten discovered a ladder propped up against the outside wall of the house. Always more adventurous than her brother, she climbed it. While exploring the roof, she went skydiving, tumbling down the chimney—just like the jolly old elf himself. Laura heard desperate meows coming from the fireplace. Sleepy and puzzled at the late hour, she opened the flue and out rolled the kitten!

Laura said, "I have to name her Sandy Claws." The women took the opportunity to bring Sandy inside, then they retrapped her golden tabby brother. Sandy's brother didn't react to any of the names they tried on him, until Matagot—a ferocious cat-spirit from France—gained his attention. So, he became known as Matagot Krampuss.

Even with her young kittens in lockdown, Mama continued to come by for food and clean water. She sat in the warmth of the evening sun against the house. Extending an olive branch for the betrayal of trapping, Laura sat on the deck and spoke to her. Mama Kitty accepted the apology by slowly blinking her eyes.

For the most part, Mama Kitty was a restless soul—always on the move. Whether from fear or distrust or a cat's natural need to always search for food, Mama Kitty never sat still more than a few moments at a time. "This life was hers, but we were allowed to visit," Marcia said.

Months passed and the kittens thrived, but the women worried about the mother. She didn't seem right. By then, the weather had turned hot and dry. Marcia set out water and made sure there was plenty of food, but Mama Kitty visits grew farther and farther apart. When they managed to spot her, she moved slowly, painfully. The uneaten food grew rancid. Then one day, Mama Kitty failed to show up at all. Something was definitely wrong.

Mama Kitty wasn't the only one going through a tough time. Laura awaited back surgery. In the meantime, her knees throbbed. Despite her discomfort, she still ventured outside for a few minutes of private time with her thoughts, while keeping a watchful eye out for Mama Kitty. The vigil for Mama Kitty seemed to give her more purpose. Yet for several days, the wanderer failed to appear. One evening, Laura saw her; Mama Kitty sat motionless in the twilight. That wasn't like her at all.

Marcia loves an old Scottish proverb that said, "There are three steps between Heaven and Earth, and in some places, even less." It reminds her to hesitate before walking into half-light, twilight or misty places because you might go in too deep and wind up completely on the other side.

"Cats are never fully in this world, and even less so at dusk," Marcia said.

In the past, as her cats are taking their final steps in this life, Marcia has watched them walk through the half-light, where the solid form of the living and the translucence of the ghostly appear to be the same. She describes the half-light effect as if someone painted a watercolor of the yard, and then painted another watercolor of a little tabby cat on top of that.

"I've seen my cats in the half-light when they let me know they're passing on," Marcia said. "Each time it happened I'd be willing to swear they were solid in-the-world cats . . . except for something different about them that I still cannot explain."

When Laura saw Mama Kitty, it was one of those suspended moments when time seems to stretch for a long moments, then she realized only a few seconds had passed. The cat was simply no longer there. Laura had never seen a ghost cat before, but on several occasions she had felt them rub up against her.

A few minutes later, she came inside and told Marcia, "I saw Mama Kitty out there." Marcia had just come inside and hadn't seen her. A sensation, like a delicate feather, touched in her mind at Laura's words. A very subtle alarm went off.

That night, Laura saw Mama Kitty in a dream. The tabby leaned her face forward and head-bumped Laura, the way cats do when they're saying, "You're family."

The next morning, some invisible force drew Marcia outside. For no particular reason, she got up from the table, went into the backyard, and headed to the back of the house to a disused narrow strip of grass with invading blackberries. There she found Mama Kitty stretched out on her side with her eyes closed. She had passed away several days earlier. An old wound in her back leg, the source of the limp, was the suspected killer. Marcia felt sad but not surprised, especially after the omens. She hoped Mama Kitty had died in her sleep.

As they buried her in the backyard close to the spot where she liked to sit and sun herself, they thanked her for her kittens, who were growing up safe and loved inside the house.

Today, Mama Kitty's feline legacies have matured into healthy, loving and safe housecats, although it took a long time for them to warm up. The women believe Mama Kitty was telling Laura it was okay, that they were taking good care of her kittens. She understood now the women were trying to help them.

"Cats don't quite go away," Marcia said. "Not if they don't want to. Sometimes it's a shadow with stripes, or a sensation on the skin. Sometimes my indoor tabby, who adopted the kittens, would turn her head at the right moment, and I would think to myself, 'Oh!' Another cat will chirp or start purring without any reason. At least, not reason to my eyes. Yet, even as a ghost, Mama Kitty does not stay. She is Kipling's Cat."

*****

Marcia Wilson is a Pacific Northwest resident, illustrator, and writer. She has always had cats in her life.

Bright as Moonshine

Moonshine came into Bernadette Cheek's life the day he was born in 1978, an offspring of Bernadette's female cat. Bernadette's younger sister claimed the longhaired kitten with green eyes, who, as a bonus, came with extra toes on his front paws. Sis named him Moonshine because he was all white, like the moon. After all five of the kids had grown up and moved away, Moonshine stayed with Mom and Dad, who lived a mile from Bernadette in Northern

California.

In 1992, Mom found a rambunctious stray Siberian Husky getting soaked in a heavy rainstorm. She brought him home. They named him Shep. It wasn't long before Shep and Moonshine became a four-legged odd couple. They were better than best friends; they were wrestling buddies. If they had joined the World Wrestling Entertainment (WWE), they might have named their team The Beasts.

But nothing from the WWE could beat the action of the gentle canine-feline smackdowns. For years, the pair enjoyed their bouts. Shep was surprisingly gentle with his older teammate.

One afternoon in 1998, when Moonshine was approaching twenty years old, Shep accidentally landed a body avalanche on the elderly cat, injuring his hind leg. Mom and Dad rushed him to the veterinarian. It was a good news/bad news situation. Bad news: Moonshine broke his leg. Good news: It was a simple fracture; it should heal. The vet set the leg and put it in a cast. He prescribed cage rest and a quiet environment—wrestling was out. Mom and Dad complied, confining him to a small bathroom. Moonshine, a very social kitty, languished in isolation, so instead they put him in a cage, moving it wherever his family assembled.

When it came time to monitor Moonshine's progress, X-rays showed the bone had not properly healed. Since he was healthy before the accident, it was decided to surgically stabilize the leg. Moonshine went to surgery and the vet pinned the break.

At home it was back to caged exile. At first, the elderly cat recovered well. The cage had room enough to eat and use the litter box. That worked for a while, although Moonshine hated being confined. Then the combination of his age, the surgery, and confinement took its toll on him; Moonshine became depressed, refusing to eat or drink in his cage. He lost weight. It was obvious something else was going on. Blood work showed that his kidneys were failing. He needed someone to give him subcutaneous fluids. The vet taught Bernadette how to inject sterile fluids under Moonshine's skin, so her parents decided Moonshine would do better at Bernadette's home.

Every day Bernadette freed him from his cage for love and lap sitting, but he got restless and wanted to roam around the house. For a short time his condition improved, but then he declined rapidly. While being away from Shep helped prevent further injury, he missed his canine friend. Eventually his organs began to shut down.

Moonshine returned to Mom and Dad's house, but he wasn't the same. He had free access to the entire house. His leg had healed, but it wasn't as strong as it should have been. The dog, sensing something wasn't right, kept his distance and didn't bother his friend.

One night about four months after Moonshine's accident, Bernadette joined her parents for dinner. Moonshine was having an especially rough night. Over the previous week, he had grown thin and lethargic, uninterested in neither people nor the dog. He never moved from his spot on the floor. That night lying by the fireplace, he watched the family but didn't interact with anyone. Bernadette knew this was it. Moonshine would soon cross the Rainbow Bridge.

When Bernadette approached him, he perked up a bit. He opened his eyes and lifted his head when she spoke to him, but otherwise didn't move as Bernadette stroked his head. He purred for her.

Before Bernadette left for the evening, she hugged him and told him she loved him. She went home sad about Moonshine's future.

At precisely two a.m. that night, Bernadette was awakened by fur brushing up against her face. Then a soft voice called her name. Startled, she gasped and sat straight up in bed. Floating over her bed at eye level was Moonshine. His soft image glowed white. The voice told her, "Thank you for everything you have done for me. I love you, but I must go. It is my time."

She only had a moment to respond, "You are welcome. I love you. Goodbye." Then as she stared at him, he rose upward and vanished. The encounter was brief, ten seconds at most.

Moonshine had visited her in his last few seconds, just as he crossed over, leaving his earthly body behind.

She thought about her experience. Bernadette's heart ached, but at least she had the chance to say goodbye. She felt honored he took the time to thank her.

Bernadette's parents called the next morning to share the sad news about Moonshine. She told them she already knew. Losing Moonshine after twenty years broke her heart, but she was thankful he was no longer in pain or feeling miserable. She knew he now had a fantastic new life and had reunited with his mom and siblings.

She knows animals communicate with people. Humans just need to listen and be open to hearing them.

"We always miss our animals," she said. "In hindsight, I wouldn't have advocated to have the surgery. I'd have made different decisions. Each of our animals is revered. None of them would give up their post or duty to the family, and we have to assure them it's okay to move on. We have to help them do that."

The Incorporeal Couch Potato

Kimberly's first encounter with a cat ghost happened in 1991, although she didn't even realize it.

Several months earlier Kimberly and her husband got the world's best cat, Sebastian. The gelatinous giant had such a gentle nature; Kimberly had no doubt that her big teddy bear would be a doting uncle to their soon-to-be-born baby.

When Kimberly or her husband came home from work, they often found Sebastian sitting like a human on the sofa with his hind legs stretched out in front of him, leaning back with his front leg resting on the arm of the couch. Thirty-pound Sebastian only needed a beer, a remote control, and a slice of piping hot pizza and he would have been ready to watch Sunday night football.

Kimberly and her fur baby watched TV together all the time. Not ironically, they were both big fans of the paranormal thriller *The X-Files*.

With Sebastian sitting in his couch potato position, Kimberly often sang a little Italian tune with words she made up, "Sebas-tee-oh-ne, Sebas-tee-oh-ne, with two cute eyes and a wittle button nose." He responded by blinking his eyes slowly and purring, as if he truly understood how much love and admiration were in Kimberly's melody. As the room filled with her notes, he stared at her with an adoring expression, his lips drawn back so far it looked as if he was smiling at her. He even leaned toward Kimberly when she got to the part about a button nose, as if to say, "You see it, right?"

When Kimberly brought her first son, Corey, home from the hospital, there were complications. The preemie baby with immature lungs was vulnerable to everything, and his sensitivity to animal dander was off the charts. His doctor recommended keeping the cat away from him.

Easier said than done. Uncle Sebastian wanted to be involved in child-rearing, including protecting the infant from hungry aardvarks. The only way to do that was sleep in the crib next to him. One morning, Sebastian, with all his happy bulk, jumped in, almost toppling the crib, baby and all. Afraid Sebastian might accidentally hurt the baby, Kimberly's husband, Johnny, put the plus-size strictly inside cat (as well as their other two kitties) on the front porch—just until they could figure out a safe place for them to hang out.

A short while later, Kimberly was suddenly awakened by an overwhelming sense of panic. She felt as if someone had punched her in the belly. Sebastian was in trouble. Something horrible had happened to him. She knew it down in the depths of her soul.

She told her husband, "Something's wrong with Sebastian. Bring him inside. Hurry!"

Johnny stared at Kimberly, puzzled. At the time, Kimberly thought the look was because he believed she was overacting, but in truth, Johnny knew something Kimberly didn't know yet. She was right; Sebastian was not okay.

Earlier that morning, Kimberly's sister, Rita (who lived across the street), showed up on their porch and told Johnny, "You better come over. Sebastian's dead." She'd found Sebastian's lifeless body in the road. Rather than telling Kimberly, they quickly put together a makeshift coffin and buried him with flowers on Rita's property, agreeing it would be best to let Kimberly believe Sebastian had taken up residence at a neighbor's home.

Not knowing Sebastian's real fate, Kimberly ran outside, calling Sebastian's name over and over. Of course, he didn't respond. Every five minutes she called him from the front porch—still no Sebastian. She scoured the area, poking through garages, utility sheds, under bushes, and inside car engines, but no Sebastian.

Johnny kept reassuring her that her big boy was okay. After searching the neighborhood, she slumped down at the dining room table sobbing uncontrollably. Johnny sat beside her. Kimberly could only say, "He's dead! He's gone! God, please bring him back!"

The plan to spare Kimberly the anguish of Sebastian's death had backfired. Every day for almost a week, Kimberly combed the neighborhood, calling for Sebastian. Each time, Johnny hoped she'd give up. But she didn't. Finally, Johnny could watch her suffer no longer. When it became obvious she wasn't buying the missing cat story, he asked her to sit down. "I can't do it anymore." Johnny confessed the whole thing.

Finally, Kimberly knew what her heart had already told her. If

Johnny could have taken the pain for her, he would have. Distraught, inconsolable, she felt the gut punch again—as if she had lost a child. "I was more hurt that they kept it from me," she said. "It denied me closure. I didn't get to hold him or tell him goodbye."

Every day Kimberly prayed to God to send Sebastian back to her, somehow.

Two months after Sebastian's spirit left his body in the road, Kimberly could barely say his name without breaking down. She sat alone, watching television from the living room sofa. Outside, her sister Toni and boyfriend LJ walked along the driveway when LJ glanced inside the house through the living room window.

He turned to Toni and said, "I didn't know your sister had an inside cat."

"She doesn't."

LJ didn't believe her. He clearly saw Kimberly with an enormous black and white cat lounging behind her shoulders on the back of the sectional sofa. Oddly, the cat, with a black spot on his nose, used the wall as a backrest.

Beyond a doubt, although LJ had never met Sebastian, he described him perfectly, from his button nose to the end of his tail.

After the date, Toni told Kimberly about LJ's experience.

LJ's vision was a sign that Kimberly's prayer had been answered, just not the way she had hoped. But she never felt for an instant anything out of the ordinary. No goosebumps, chills, warm feelings. Even though she didn't see him, Sebastian had come back, laying behind her on the back of the couch just like the old days.

The emotional wounds from Sebastian's death still felt so fresh and raw, as if it had happened that day. LJ's vision was bittersweet. Kimberly couldn't hide her disappointment that Sebastian hadn't shown himself to her—yet she felt happy that he was still around.

"I felt such relief that he was still with me. It was big for me," she said.

Sebastian wasn't done, though. Many years after LJ's experience, Kimberly's then-nine-year-old son, Justin, glanced toward the laundry room. He saw a black and white cat laying by a laundry basket on the floor. When he went to pet the cat, it wasn't there. He told his mom and described the kitty. It was Sebastian, right down to the spot on the nose. Like the encounter with LJ, Justin never knew the legendary kitty. Justin arrived many years after Sebastian's road accident.

It couldn't have been one of their live feline family members, either; at the time they had no black and white cats.

It's been more than thirty years since Sebastian passed. Kimberly still misses him. At least she knows his spirit lives on. Nobody has seen him in several decades. But that doesn't mean he's not there. She often wonders if he drops in inconspicuously from time to time just to check in on them, and then moves on.

Neera

Roxana Liotta of Buenos Aires, Argentina, and her partner, Ian, shared their home with kitties Neera and Aefugusto. Although they came from the same litter, the brother and sister couldn't have looked more different.

Neera, a cream and brown tabby, had a short coat, bright yellow eyes, and white whiskers. Her brother, a handsome Maine Coon-type, was a darker, longhaired brown tabby with white whiskers and green eyes. Typically curious, Augusto often darted toward the front door when he heard noises outside. He lived a happy life until he developed kidney and stomach problems and crossed the Rainbow Bridge in May 2018 at the age of eighteen.

Shortly after Augusto's passing, Roxana and Ian, along with their other two cats, moved to a new apartment across town. The solid black siblings were named Oli, short for Olivia, and Giorgio.

In the new place, Neera liked hanging out on one of the dining room chairs. For some reason, she never showed any interest in exploring or even entering the couple's bedroom.

With three cats underfoot, Roxana had to vacuum every week to check accumulating cat hair. Whenever she vacuumed, she always kept an eye out for vibrissae, the technical term for kitty whiskers. As she moved through the apartment, she delighted anytime she discovered whiskers on the laminate flooring. Regardless of who they had belonged to, finding one made her so happy. She held onto her finds, creating an impressive whisker collection.

Shortly after Augusto passed, Neera's health began to decline. She developed chronic diarrhea. At first, the vet thought she had hyperthyroidism, but the tests came back negative. She began to experience a cascade of organ failure. Her blood pressure soared, then her kidneys began to fail. During her final year, she developed congestive heart failure.

As Neera's health plummeted, Roxana had a conversation with her kitty in which she asked Neera to return for a visit after she crossed the Rainbow Bridge.

On one of Neera's last few nights, as Ian wiped down the kitchen counter, he spotted a transparent, shapeless cat-sized haze just outside the kitchen. The vaporous form darted toward the front door—just as Augusto had done when he was alive. As it approached the door, it dissipated into nothingness.

Ian told Roxana about his sighting. Both immediately suspected Augusto was hanging around waiting for his sister to join him.

Augusto was right. Soon after his appearance, Neera stopped eating. A visit to the vet confirmed that Neera's body was shutting down. Roxana took the day off from work so she could devote those final hours to Neera. Neera spent much of the day sleeping on her favorite dining room chair. Other times, she napped on the floor. Her legs weren't cooperating, but a couple of times she struggled to take some steps. When Roxana sat on the floor, Neera leaned her head against her human's leg. They enjoyed their remaining moments together. Too soon, six o'clock came and Roxana returned Neera to the veterinarian's office. The elderly cat felt cold, so the vet instructed Roxana to keep her warm and return in the morning if she didn't improve.

During the walk home, Roxana thought she heard Neera meow through the carrier mesh, but it was impossible to be certain above the noise of the road traffic. Along the way, Roxana worked up a bit of a sweat, so she took off her sweater and placed it inside the carrier, hoping her scent would comfort Neera. When Roxana arrived at their apartment, she unzipped the carrier. Roxana took a sharp breath; Neera had died just ten days short of her twentieth birthday.

Neera had spared Roxana the pain of making a difficult decision or forever associating her new apartment with her kitty's death. "It was better for me that way, and I appreciated the wisdom in her choice," Roxana said.

Later that night Roxana and Ian buried Neera with a letter and a toy heart in a lush green flower-covered garden at Roxana's mom's house.

Roxana and Ian still had all-black Oli and Giorgio. Like the rest of their bodies, their whiskers were black.

Eight days after her passing, Neera entered Roxana's dream. She looked beautiful, full of light and a little chubby, just as she appeared in her prime. "She was letting me know she was okay," Roxana said. She thought the dream was Neera saying goodbye, but the kitty wasn't ready for her final exit yet.

Six days after her dream, Roxana was vacuuming when she came upon a white whisker on the bedroom floor. Since Neera had never shown any interest in going into that room, Roxana knew this was a clear sign. A few days later, another white whisker appeared close to the bedroom door. It was impossible for any of Neera's white whiskers to have remained in the apartment after she had vacuumed thoroughly several times since Neera's passing. Roxana felt blessed to know her sweet kitty was still with them somehow.

A few days later, Ian was again tidying the kitchen counter after dinner. He felt a friendly feline presence in the kitchen and heard the faint pitter-patter of a cat walking on a hard surface. Out of the corner of his eye, he saw a dark cat-sized form moving along on the floor. It walked into the kitchen, passed behind him, and went to the laundry area where the litter boxes are kept. The apparition was so solid and full-bodied, Ian was positive it was their live girl kitty, Oli. While the image only lasted an instant, the padding of the paws on the floor continued for several more seconds.

Ian turned on the laundry room light, expecting to see Oli, but found no cat. He quickly located her sleeping soundly on the bed, on the opposite side of the apartment. Giorgio, who was much too large a cat to be the dark shape, had been comfortably lying on the couch next to Roxana.

Ian immediately told Roxana about his experience. Based on the ghost cat's small size, it showing up so soon after Neera's passing, and the unexplained appearance of the white whiskers, they were convinced the kitty in the kitchen was Neera.

Roxana was thrilled her little girl had decided to come say hi, and as she had hoped, Neera let her human know she was okay. Roxana's heart was filled with joy.

After that night, neither Roxana nor Ian ever saw shadows or white whiskers again. Neera's work here was done.

*****

Roxana is a cat behaviorist, animal communicator, Reiki healer, runes and tarot reader, translator, and a Norse mythology buff. She admits she is the archetypal crazy cat mom/lady who also dreams of maybe one day adopting a Pug.

"We had to install the pet door in the Pearly Gates because the cats couldn't decide if they wanted in or out."

CHAPTER 3: FAMILY REUNIONS

Feeling the weight of a cat's paws pressing into your shoulders in the middle of the night—not much beats that. —Hiro Arikawa

It's never easy to say that final goodbye—to know you're never going to hear Fluffy's purr again or snuggle next to him at night. All too often, we are denied that goodbye altogether, if he passes unexpectedly or disappears without a trace. During COVID, many of us weren't even permitted to be in the room when our pets left this life. But some cats have to get in the last word, so to speak. As we know, there's no deterring a determined cat when he wants something—such as making a final loving connection with his people.

If we're lucky they might drop by for a closing visit. If we're truly blessed, we may enjoy periodic appearances for many years.

The Paper Pusher

Pyewacket came into Ruth McClure's life in 1973 already named, when a fellow nurse discovered her child was allergic to their new Siamese kitten. Faced with the choice of a kid with a chronically snotty nose or finding the kitten a new home, the mom had to do the latter. Ruth didn't have a pet at the time and offered to take the Meezer.

The kitten was stunning; her brown—almost black—seal point face was a compromise between the old-fashioned apple-headed Siamese and the new-style wedge shape; an oval face but with the pointy nose. As she aged, her beige body transformed to a dark brown.

Even as a kitten, Pyewacket loved to carry on lengthy conversations. She often sat on Ruth's lap, looked into her human's face, and shared her thoughts in that strident Siamese meow. Ruth answered, and the conversation volleyed back and forth indefinitely, usually with Ruth tiring before Pyewacket. Whenever Pyewacket wanted something, she wasn't shy about asking, either. If her verbal requests were ignored, she found more direct ways to communicate.

Ruth was a nurse anesthetist at a large Dallas hospital, working twenty-four-hour shifts. With seven kids all needing something, housekeeping tasks sometimes fell to the bottom of her to-do list—perpetually. Unfortunately, Pyewacket's litter box frequently received less attention than the Siamese thought it should.

One particular day, when the box had been neglected, Pyewacket had had enough. Ruth climbed into bed for some badly-needed rest after her latest one-day shift when she felt the cat jump on the bed and tread next to her face. Ruth opened her eyes to find herself nose-to-nose with Pyewacket, who held a petrified cat turd in her mouth. The cat deposited the poop on the king-size pillow next to Ruth's face, as if to say, "Get up and clean my box!" Thanks to Pyewacket's exceptional communication skills, Ruth never neglected the litter box again.

Eventually Ruth converted her spare bedroom into a combination library/office. Whenever she needed to use the computer or had time to work on her novel, she went into the library. Naturally, Pyewacket joined her. Three or four times a week, office manager Pyewacket monitored the goings on from beneath Ruth's desk, where the cat liked to rub against her legs.

Decades before wireless computer accessories, cables snaked their way from Ruth's computer to her then-state-of-the-art dot-matrix tractor-fed printer. Whenever Ruth printed her manuscript, the tractor fed the perforated paper in jerky movements that flowed out into a tidy, folded stack on the other side. On those exciting days when the printer suddenly sprang to life, Pyewacket sat under the endless sheet of printer paper. As the paper exited the printer and settled into a pile on the other side, Pyewacket worked her way beneath the paper, stuck her foot under the edge and swatted with her paw. She took great delight in protecting Ruth from the undulating paper monster

From Ruth's higher vantage point, the continuous paper sheets mysteriously popped up and rustled on their own. Sometimes, with feline help, those tidy stacks of printed paper turned into high haphazard heaps. Pyewacket kept up her antics for the rest of her life.

During Pyewacket's twenty-third year, as her health had begun to wane, Ruth knew the time was approaching when she'd have to say goodbye.

Pyewacket had been a strictly indoor cat her entire life. Ruth's home backed up to a creek and she didn't want any of the predators that hung out near the water to have Siamese for dinner. But one afternoon while Ruth was away running chores, Pyewacket talked Ruth's then-husband into letting her go outside.

An hour later, Ruth returned home and learned of Pyewacket's excursion. As Ruth combed the neighborhood for Pye, their next-door neighbor pulled into her driveway. The woman told Ruth she had found Pyewacket wandering outside and took her to the vet for IV fluids. The vet said she was a very old cat and it would be best to euthanize her.

Ruth never understood why the woman euthanized Pyewacket rather than calling her, but it was too late. Ruth's little office companion was gone.

"I knew she was on her last legs," Ruth said. "But I would have rather taken her to the vet myself."

As a surgical anesthetist, Ruth said, "I've seen a lot of death in my life." She knew Pyewacket's passing was inevitable, and she accepted it. However, "I was very pissed at my husband for letting her outside."

After Pyewacket's death, Ruth continued working in the office twice a week, but she no longer looked forward to it; it was going to be so lonely. The next time she worked on her novel, she thought she saw a cat out of the corner of her eye. When she focused on the spot, nothing was there. Of course not. Pyewacket was her only kitty at the time. She dismissed it as a trick of light, or maybe she hadn't gotten enough sleep after her last twenty-four hour shift.

The first time she printed something after Pyewacket's passing, Ruth heard the normal grinding of the tractor feed, but she also heard something else she didn't expect—the pop of the printer paper. The paper snapped up and shimmied magically as if someone hit it from beneath. For just a moment, everything was just as it had been before Pyewacket passed. Then the next moment, the printer simply fed the paper as it was designed, rhythmically, predictably. The paper no longer acted alive.

"It startled me the first time it happened because I didn't have a cat then," Ruth recalls.

Days later, while working in her office, she glimpsed another feline image—so briefly. Once again, she was alone in the room. And as before, when she activated the printer, the paper suddenly popped from below. Ruth could almost feel Pyewacket's delight at attacking paper beast as it came to life. A few minutes later, Ruth felt a familiar sensation—a cat brushing against her leg. Automatically, she reached down to touch it, but despite the pressure against her calf, her fingers contacted nothing—no fur, no muscle.

On Pyewacket's next visit, Ruth tried to initiate a conversation, as she had so many times before. "Hi Pyewacket, whatcha doing?" Ruth held her breath and listened for the strident response, but

Pyewacket kept mum.

Early on, Pyewacket checked in whenever Ruth worked in her office. For months, every time Ruth used the printer, the paper popping continued. Then Pyewacket occasionally missed a day. The visits gradually grew less frequent and more sporadic.

Eight months after Pyewacket's passing, Ruth bought a fancy new flatbed printer. Pyewacket stopped appearing.

When Ruth looks back, she recalls that Pyewacket's final visit was her longest, maybe a couple of minutes. "She was trying to tell me she was okay and goodbye." After all, Pyewacket, too, had missed her goodbye hug.

Azlan

Even as a kid, Alex Paquet worried about homeless cats. When she was ten, a friend's dad, Dave, found a stray mom cat who made a nursery out of an old boat parked outside the company where he worked. One afternoon, while Dave was sneaking the little family some canned cat food, he showed the kittens to little Alex.

Momma was a calico. Her kittens looked like they came from an assorted candy bin: a calico girl, an orange boy, a black cutie, and one seal point Siamese kitten with gray-blue eyes. Momma cat was friendly and didn't mind people playing with the kittens. Alex fell for the blue-eyed cutie. She'd always had a thing for Siamese markings and blue eyes.

When the kittens were around eight weeks old, Dave said Alex should take her little friend home. If he was left with his mother, he would become another feral cat, Dave said, and there were already too many homeless cats on the street.

Alex named her kitten Azlan after the regal lion from the Narnia movies based on the books by C.S. Lewis. It seemed to fit him.

Azlan was a very sweet cat, and although he never liked being cuddled or held, he clearly loved his people. He willingly suffered the indignity of wearing teddy bear dresses whenever Alex played dress-up. Weaving in out of human legs, he shared scads of loose brown fur with anyone who stood still for more than a few seconds.

As affectionate as he was, he never slept with Alex on her bed. He preferred to lounge on the table in the dining room. During the day, when Alex's parents were at work and she was at school, Azlan, in a typically feline move, sought out Grandpa, who hung out on his favorite brown recliner. Azlan would lounge on the leg rest. Together, they watched television—ironic, since Grandpa claimed he didn't like cats. Sometimes Azlan lay on the floor near the entryway window to bask in the morning sun. As the day progressed, he moved a few feet now and then to keep up with the sunbeams.

Azlan, an active kitty, enjoyed dashing through the house. He was also a certified catnip addict. He couldn't resist the herb. When he got a whiff, he acted full-blown drunk, running around and clawing the floor.

He also loved his cat toys, but he never once showed interest in any toys that didn't contain catnip. He was a master of the game of hide-and-seek, mainly the hide part. He often found a secluded spot and hid for hours at a time, only appearing when he was ready to reveal himself.

The carefree kitty was not without his challenges. Because of a problem with his neuter surgery, he was prone to frequent urinary tract infections and blockages.

Two days before his third Christmas, he uncharacteristically slept on Alex's bed, something he'd never done before. In retrospect, Alex believed he knew he was dying. On the day he passed, he once again performed his great vanishing act, and died in his hiding place after Alex had fallen asleep. Alex's mom found Azlan, but didn't tell her daughter about his passing.

The next day, Alex was still in the dark about Azlan. Her parents decided they could cushion the blow with a new kitten. They called cat breeders in the area to see if anyone had any kittens. Mom finally found a Highland Lynx breeder with one seven-week-old kitten. She told the breeder it was an emergency and that Alex's cat had just passed. Mom neglected to tell her that Alex hadn't been told yet. They were going to break the news after they returned home with the new kitten.

The breeder made small talk as Alex played with the tiny cat. Unfortunately, the woman spilled the cat litter when she asked Alex how she was doing after the death of her kitty. Alex was shocked. She hated crying in front of people, but she simply couldn't hold it together.

Alex left the breeder's house with her new kitten, Tinala, and went home. Alex found herself immersed in conflicting emotions: the joy of getting a new kitten and the sudden news of Azlan's death. That was a lot for a thirteen-year-old to take in.

When she walked into the house holding her kitten, she looked toward Azlan's favorite place and there he was, sitting on the corner of the dining room table, looking right at her. By the time she looked back at the spot, he was gone. Over and over, she eyed the same spot, hoping to see him, but he had disappeared. That same night, after Alex went to bed, she felt a full-grown cat hop up on the end of her bed. When she looked she saw Azlan, although his body was vague. She didn't try to touch him—perhaps because he looked as if he existed between spaces. She enjoyed feeling the weight of his body until she fell asleep. After that night, he never came back.

Alex wasn't the slightest bit scared. In her thirteen years, she'd seen a lot of things to be scared of, but her pet cat telling her goodbye definitely wasn't one of them.

*****

Alex Paquet is a freelance artist and indie comic creator from North Carolina. She has collected a variety of paranormal experiences throughout her life, which sparked her interest in ghosts and the supernatural.

A Moment in Heaven

Isabelle is not religious at all. She's a scientist, with an analytical mind, who knows there is a logical explanation for everything.

She grew up in Europe and moved to the United States as a young adult. Back in the old country, Isabelle's mom had two cats: a seal point Siamese named Bicho, and Tiki, a brown Burmese, an ancient breed known for their copper eyes. The two cats loved hanging out in the flower garden. When her mother passed away, Isabelle brought the cats to live with her in the States. As American kitties, they were only allowed to visit the garden on a leash—and Tiki hated that leash.

Only eighteen months after trekking halfway across the world, Bicho died at the age of nineteen. Tiki had always seemed quiet and submissive to Isabelle, and lived in Bicho's shadow. But after Bicho passed, Tiki blossomed. He quickly loved being the center of attention. And it didn't take long for T, as Isabelle began to call him, to steal her heart. They were soul mates. He slept under the covers with Isabelle. He started to vocalize more, always getting the last word.

Isabelle and T had long conversations. She made a statement, then he commented back, followed by her rebuttal. As the two looped back and forth, T's commentary progressively decreased in volume; however, he always got the last word under his breath.

Eventually, T developed lymphoma. Together he and Isabelle fought the disease. When he had a bad day, Isabelle cradled him until he fell asleep. Through T's illness, Isabelle learned patience. For two years, top veterinarians treated him with the latest advances veterinary medicine had to offer. Working three jobs didn't leave much time to care for a sick kitty, so Isabelle slowed down to allow her more time with T. Toward the end, he wanted attention constantly.

At one point, Isabelle had to force twelve pills down him each day. Weak and yellow, one day he looked at her and said in his own way, "Enough!" Hard as it was to give up, Isabelle respected T's wish. That was the last time he had to take medicine.

That day they sat outside in the garden together near the flowers. T had a last chance to do all the things he loved to do: smell the plants, watch the birds and hear the leaves flutter in the breeze. This time, he didn't need a leash. The next day, they drove to the animal hospital for the last time. He was thirteen.

About six months after T died, Isabelle was in her second-floor bedroom when her new partner Paula started to close the door. For no reason, Isabelle blurted out, "Don't close the door. T is climbing up the stairs." She stopped. How bizarre that must have sounded! Paula stared at her. Isabelle was about to apologize when a transparent golden glow appeared in front of her, the same long, oval shape as the Mexican painting, Our Lady of Guadalupe. The center gleamed white.

Before she could react, the golden glow moved through her. Isabelle felt no sensation of impact, no blast of cold or warm. A profound hug engulfed her entire body in unconditional love. For just a few seconds, she felt inner peace and bliss. Then, as quickly as it had moved through her, the light and the peaceful bliss vanished. She knew it was T. After all, she had sensed him coming up the stairs.

At that moment, she understood people's near-death experiences, the beautiful light in the tunnel, the feeling of peace, joy, and love, the reluctance to return to the living. She felt like she was in the place others describe as Heaven. Does it exist? Isabelle doesn't know, but if it does, she was there, briefly.

While Paula didn't personally witness the light, she watched her partner freeze and stare at something invisible in reaction to the presence.

But that wasn't the last of T. A year or so later, a friend stayed at Isabelle's place in the same bedroom where Isabelle saw the light. The woman, an MIT scientist who absolutely did not believe in the paranormal, was awakened by the feeling of whiskers on her face. There were no cats in the house at the time. It had to be T.

Isabelle's scientist mind believes we live in one reality, but at the same time other realities in other dimensions share the same space. She explains, "When we pass, we just shift to a different dimension; that would explain ghosts, déja vu, and other paranormal events."

That said, she can't explain that glorious golden light, other than that it was Tiki hugging her goodbye.

*****

Isabelle is a musician living in Massachusetts. She has, in the past, worked with animals and is now training to be an animal communicator.

Josette

In 2003, Janice bought her first home, a small condo outside of Boston, Massachusetts. At the age of forty-eight, it was the first time in her life she had lived alone. Before then, she'd always had roommates. Finally, she could shut the door to her one-bedroom apartment knowing she was the only one at home! No noise; no interruptions. Since the condo association allowed pets, she decided it was time to adopt one.

As much as she loved dogs, after a year, she decided to adopt a cat instead. After all, cats are more convenient for condo living. So, the search was on for her kitty companion.

She visited some local shelters. In the get-to-know-you room, she felt like she had been dropped into the tale of Goldilocks. All the candidates were too big, too mean, or too hissy. Some didn't like to be held, others totally ignored her.

After interviewing kitties for months with no good matches, a local shelter called to tell her they had a very sweet female cat. The declawed cat had been found wandering around in the woods, very likely dumped. Janice jumped in her car and rushed to meet the new arrival.

She turned out to be a small, medium-haired black cat. A black cat wasn't really what Janice had in mind. She wasn't superstitious, but she wanted a cat with some color, like a tabby. All her doubts vanished, though, when she held the kitty. The little black cat didn't scratch, bite, or hiss like the others. She liked being held. In that instant they bonded. Janice told the shelter volunteer, "Mine!"

According to the records, the cat was between three and five years old. She thought, "Great! I'll have her for a long time."

Her foster caregiver had named her Lumpkin, after a horse from *The Lord of the Rings*, but that was no name for a sweet, beautiful cat. Janice named her Josette, after the love interest of vampire Barnabas Collins in the late 1960s gothic soap opera *Dark Shadows*.

On her first day away from her new pet, Janice returned from work to find Josette shaking, foaming at the mouth, and drooling. "She's having a seizure!" she thought.

Janice cleaned Josette up. Suddenly the foaming and trembling stopped. She wasn't having a seizure; she was just afraid of being abandoned again. She did that to a much lesser degree almost every day after Janice returned home from work. Whenever Janice entered the house, she found Josette drooling and shaking a little because she was happy to see her.

Janice and Josette fell into a comfortable routine. They took naps together and at night Josette jumped on the bed near Janice's head. Janice held her paw for a few minutes. Satisfied and safe, Josette got up and walked to Janice's feet. There, she'd curl up and to go to sleep. In the morning, Josette woke Janice by gently pulling at her hair with her teeth. Sometimes they cuddled, and Josette wrapped her paws around Janice's neck. Such a sweetie!

Once, when Janice was trying to take an after-work nap, Josette kept jumping on her back to get her up. Her message was clear: "Pay attention to me! Dinner is late!"

Janice and Josette had a very special mental connection. Josette liked to hide behind the couch to take a nap. After she hadn't seen her cat for a while, Janice thought, "Josette, Josette, come on out!" A few minutes later she appeared from behind the couch. This wasn't just a coincidence; it happened many times. Janice would just think, "Come out" and the black kitty showed up.

For such a youngster, Josette didn't have much energy. She'd play for a minute or two, then lose interest. Health issues cropped up—more than normal in a five-year-old. Janice had to take her to the vet a couple of times a year for one issue or another. Her teeth were in such rough shape; she even needed some extractions.

When Janice asked the vet why such a young cat would be getting sick so often and didn't like to play, he told her, "This is an old cat. She's between ten and thirteen years old." Wow! Instead of an expected ten years ahead of them, it looked like they'd have five, maybe fewer. The time didn't matter, though. Janice loved her senior girl so much; they'd enjoy whatever time awaited them.

After three years, Janice noticed Josette had lost weight. The vet delivered the grim news: Little Josette had cancer. Janice didn't want to put such a fragile kitty through the stress of surgery or chemo, so she managed Josette's pain and kept an eye on her quality of life. She knew it was time to say goodbye when Josette stopped eating and cleaning herself.

At the vet's office, Janice stroked Josette softly. She reminded her what a good kitty she was, how much she loved her, and soon she'd get her claws back. Then it was over. Janice was devastated. She had Josette cremated and kept her ashes in the living room.

But like her supernatural namesake, Josette would not stay gone. One afternoon, long after Josette's passing, Janice was in her bedroom brushing her hair when out of the corner of her eye she saw a flicker of light in the hallway. *That's odd!* She put down her brush and went to the hall to investigate.

Leisurely trotting down the ten-foot-long hallway was Josette, facing forward with her graceful ebony face, and her long, solid body as she moved past Janice. Janice stared, eyes wide, fearing if she blinked Josette would be gone. All too soon, Josette walked into the bathroom then disappeared. In all, they had maybe fifteen seconds together—not nearly enough time. Janice wondered, "What did I just see?"

Over the next few months, Janice tried to convince herself that Josette's appearance didn't happen, but she finally concluded that some higher power had sent her kitty back to visit her. As if in confirmation, some months later, Josette returned, but this time not as a fully formed animal. While Janice watched TV in the living room, she saw an opaque, scraggly black ball shoot out from under the ottoman and disappear. This encounter lasted only a few seconds.

Another time, Janice was in her bedroom putting away laundry when, out of the corner of her eye, she saw that same black ball jump on her bed, then leap into the air and dissolve. As before, it happened so quickly it seemed almost imperceptible.

Josette visited Janice one final time in 2018. While prepping the condo for new hardwood floors, Janice had to pack everything up in boxes. After the workers finished the floors, Janice had to unpack all her belongings. Without thinking, she placed a box on Josette's favorite sleeping chair. As she bent over to unpack the box, she felt a cat jump upon her back and then spring off.

Since Josette was the only cat she'd had, Janice had no doubt who the black ball was and who bounced off her. "Ghosts don't like change," she said. "And I guess the same goes for ghost cats!"

Josette hasn't been back since. Janice said she wasn't scared. She felt happy and blessed that her beautiful Josette loved her enough to come back to visit.

Smoky Bear

Jane Watkins admits she's the epitome of the crazy cat lady. The Dallas-based accountant has had kitties since the 1980s; she's loved them all. But one longhaired kitten who was weaned too early won her heart above all others.

In 1999, a friend told Jane about a pair of eight-week-old kittens she'd been fostering for a rescue group in Rockwall, Texas. The male was a solid black Maine Coon-mix with a smoky gray undercoat; his sister by another mother was a tortoiseshell. Both kittens were healthy and adorable, and Jane couldn't resist them. Before long, she brought them both home and had them neutered. She named the male Smoky Bear because he looked like a little bear cub. Much of the time, she just called him Smoky. Anyone who has been around tortoiseshells knows how Diva got her name. She had tortitude to spare.

From day one, the kittens slept with Jane. Diva always claimed the high ground next to Jane's face, but the moment Diva vacated the spot, Smoky seized the favored position. When Diva was in her spot, Smoky curled up next to Jane's legs. While he could walk gracefully, at times he moved like a bulldozer. Sometimes, to get to just the right place, he plowed across her legs or feet. Smoky was a sound sleeper; He could sleep through anything—even the most violent North Texas thunderstorms.

The big male may have been dumber than a box of hair, but he loved everyone, especially his girls—his tortoiseshell companion and his human. Diva adored him too—that is, until she didn't. At times, Diva tired of all his attention. When she ran out of patience, the claws came out and she smacked him. The gentle giant never fought back.

Diva, on the other paw, was high strung. Jane believed her nervous nature was due to the mini quakes occurring in the Dallas area at that time caused by fracking.

As gentle and loving as Smoky Bear was, he was a card-carrying member of the naughty kitty club. A feline wrecking ball, he could destroy every breakable item in the house. He had a particular talent for demolishing wine glasses. To accomplish this, he jumped on the kitchen counters and knocked down the stemware hanging from a rack under Jane's upper cabinets. He chewed up cords too; Jane couldn't count the number of phone cords she had to replace.

Despite his wake of destruction, Jane couldn't stay mad at Smoky. She cherished those times he sat with his butt in her lap while resting his paws on her chest. "He'd just sit and stare at me with love in his eyes," Jane said. "After all, the eyes are the windows to the soul."

In his prime, Smoky topped the scales at eighteen pounds. When he leaped up on the foot of the bed, the mattress gave way under his weight. As he aged beyond his peak, though, Smoky lost much of his impressive bulk. In 2013, the health of both kitties began to decline; they were both diagnosed with kidney disease. The vet prescribed subcutaneous fluids twice a week for both cats.

The big guy was a model patient. As a reward, after each treatment, Jane spoiled him with treats and pets. But Diva wasn't having any of it; she was combative and uncooperative. Jane had to let nature take its course. For the rest of their lives, Smoky and Diva went to the vet twice a year for blood work.

Health problems piled on. Diva developed high blood pressure, and all the painful conditions that go along with it. Treatment for hypertension requires a daily pill, and as with the subcutaneous fluids, every single dose turned into a battle. Without the medicine, her blood pressure soared. Jane made the difficult decision to let Diva go right before Thanksgiving of 2016.

When his girlfriend failed to come home, poor Smoky wondered what happened. For a few days, he searched the house for her, repeatedly checking her favorite places and calling for her. For the first few weeks after her passing, he was extra clingy.

Six weeks after Diva's passing, Jane got another cat. The arrival was an eleven-year-old matron who Jane brought home on Martin Luther King Day in 2017. Angelica, a dainty black cat with a couple of tiny white patches on her chest and belly, had belonged to one of Jane's coworkers. Living in a clowder of five, the friend couldn't give her the attention she needed and she was bullied by his other cats. Rehoming her seemed like the kindest option.

With his new girlfriend by his side, Smoky Bear was happy again. The newcomer claimed Diva's old sleeping spot in a little cat bed next to Jane's pillow. Smoky Bear resumed sleeping by Jane's side.

A year after Diva passed, the vet discovered a tumor in Smoky's belly. The cancer was already advanced and painful. Jane decided it wasn't in Smoky's best interest to wait. That day in August 2017, after eighteen happy years, Smoky joined his companion Diva across the Rainbow Bridge.

Jane loved him and missed him. Even with Angelica around, the house seemed empty.

A couple of weeks after his passing in the middle of the night, Jane woke up by the feeling of the bed dipping deeply—as if a very large cat had jumped onto the mattress. At first she worried that an intruder may have entered her home. She wondered, "Did I lock my doors?"

If it wasn't human, it had to be feline. A quick glance found no cat at her feet. She knew it wasn't Angelica. She was a tiny thing; she couldn't have made the mattress move like that. Besides, Angelica had already settled into bed next to Jane's face, snoring loudly.

Whatever it was had already gone.

"It's comforting thinking it was him," Jane said. "I missed him a lot. He was so lovable."

Jane, a Christian, believes there are spirits and angels all around us. Sometimes they manifest through our pets. "I think you're more open during that twilight time between waking and sleep," she said. She got the impression Smoky wanted to make sure she was okay.

Although Smoky isn't a regular visitor, she feels him in bed occasionally, although less often these days than right after he passed. Over the four years since he's been gone, he's shown up half a dozen times. It's always the same—in bed in the middle of the night Jane feels the pressure against her legs. By the time she wakes up enough to look down, he's already gone. Sometimes she feels him clumsily stomp on her foot in bed, just as he had done years before. Other times he's graceful.

Jane recalls his last visit occurred in 2020. "It doesn't happen all the time. I think he's still around, for now. I don't feel his presence as often as I used to, just every so often. He might come back; he might not. I don't know. I leave myself open to that. Animals are with us even after they're gone. Spiritually we're all connected."

*****

Jane Watkins is a lifelong cat lover and cat owner, and freely admits to being a crazy cat lady (without owning twenty cats.) She lives in Dallas with her kitties Angelica and Walter White, aka Wally Boo.

Iris

JaneA Kelley grew up immersed in metaphysical ideas, but when it came to paranormal experiences, she was a skeptic. She'd seen too many New Age followers who blindly accepted the latest idea to show up on the *New York Times* bestseller list. Blind belief wasn't in JaneA's nature.

JaneA's mother owned and operated a metaphysical shop that sold books, crystals, tarot cards, and incense. As a kid, when she helped out at the store, she read lots of books on spiritual and supernatural phenomena. She practiced spirituality too. But when it came to ghosts and the afterlife, she had to see something to believe it. She wanted proof. The idea of ghost cats certainly never entered her mind.

When JaneA was a teenager, the family went to the local animal shelter because her younger brother wanted a dog. They came home with an Old English Sheepdog mix named Ruffle . . . and two three-month-old kittens. Iris was a diminutive shorthaired calico with gold-green eyes and Purr Bear was a longhaired black and white Maine Coon mix.

JaneA and Iris developed a special bond. JaneA midwifed several litters of Iris' kittens. (Hey, it was the 1980s and in rural Maine. Spay/neuter wasn't a thing yet.) JaneA and Iris also had a special psychic connection. One early autumn day in 1994, JaneA planned a walk in the woods to check out a turkey nesting area several hundred yards away. To hide her presence from the turkeys, she made her way around the edge of the forest. Just as she was about to set off into the woods, she turned around and there stood Iris. "Go away," she whispered to the cat. "You're going to scare the birds." Iris looked at her as if to say, "Are you serious?" And when it became clear she wasn't going anywhere, JaneA told her, "Okay, Iris, lead the way!"

Watching wildlife takes stealthy motion and light feet—something JaneA didn't share with Iris. Every time JaneA snapped a twig or crunched dried leaves beneath her shoes, Iris shot her a look. It was as if Iris thought, "No wonder humans are such lousy hunters." JaneA couldn't believe it when Iris guided her through the woods right to the turkeys' nesting area! That was a very special moment between them. How did Iris know where JaneA wanted to go?

The years passed, and JaneA eventually went away to college. After college, she returned to her hometown and got her own apartment near her mom's place. Nineteen years after their trip to the animal shelter, it was clear Iris was nearing the end of her life. She just got slower . . . and slower. She ate less, and finally not at all. JaneA recalls that sometimes Iris acted like she was between worlds.

Halloween, 1999, JaneA knew Iris was dying and she didn't want to miss the opportunity to say goodbye, so she stopped at Mom's house on her way to a Halloween party. JaneA knelt beside the chair where her mother sat. Iris lay on her lap, curled up in blankets. JaneA stroked her head and thanked her for all the amazing experiences they shared. Then she headed out the door and off to the party. After the party, JaneA swung by to see if Mom was okay and if Iris was still alive.

As JaneA walked through the mud room and into the kitchen, she saw Iris's head peeking out from under the tablecloth on the kitchen table. JaneA knew those gold-green eyes. They made eye contact for a moment, then Iris ducked back into the darkness under the table. JaneA's first thought was, "Wow, Iris looks a lot more alive than she did when I left!"

"Iris is looking pretty spry," she said to her mother.

"Iris died two hours ago," Mom told her.

JaneA shared with her mother what she had just seen—a full-body apparition of Iris—and Mom said, "I guess she stayed around to say goodbye to you."

While JaneA felt sad about Iris's passing, she also felt honored that her old friend had stayed around long enough for a last goodbye.

Before that night, JaneA was skeptical of the paranormal. "I'll believe it if I see it," she always told herself. "Well, I saw it, and now I believe it!"

*****

JaneA Kelley is an award-winning author and blogger, and a professional member of the Cat Writers' Association. She is currently working on a memoir which, of course, features cats doing cool things.

Phoebe

It's tough to lose a cat at any age, but with advances in veterinary medicine, twelve was just too young, especially for Joanne Anderson's first forever kitty, Phoebe. The Babylon, New York, third grade teacher grew up a dog person. Because the family had several

Afghan Hounds with tremendous prey drive, she could only offer temporary refuge to special-needs kittens from the animal shelter. The foster babies were safety separated from the hounds in their own special kitten room. They came and went with regular frequency.

At four weeks old, Phoebe came to Joanne from the local shelter along with her handsome brother and another unrelated boy. The three bundles of fluff still needed bottle feeding.

With Joanne's painstaking care, the trio grew into healthy, weaned kittens. The two boys were adopted into separate homes. The little girl had a harder time. Over the next few weeks, three potential homes fell through for Phoebe, a beautiful longhair tuxedo. After the third family didn't work out, the temporary kitten became a permanent resident. By then, the dog situation had resolved itself. Alfie, the more aggressive Afghan, had died, and Juliet, the grand dame in cancer remission, had mellowed significantly.

When Phoebe reached full size, Joanne picked out an aqua safety cat collar with rhinestones to match Phoebe's elegant personality. A heart-shaped name tag with Phoebe's name and Joanne's phone number dangled from the D-ring. The collar fit perfectly—tight enough not to slip off over her head, but loose enough to slide a couple of fingers beneath. The safety catch was designed to spring open if the collar became entangled, but that was never necessary.

When it came to appropriate scratching places, Phoebe never got the memo. Even though Joanne scattered cat scratchers throughout the house, Phoebe ignored them all in favor of an old running shoe. After she started scratching on the outside of the shoe, there was no going back.

Phoebe's life touched all of Joanne's remaining pets. She managed to peacefully coexist with the remaining Afghans. She immediately welcomed Alan, an enormous black Afghan hound, a refugee from the Oyster Bay Shelter, by lying beside him and tickling his enormous feet with her paws. She was a loving and protective big sister to Jerry, a kitten with congenital liver problems. He only grew to about two pounds, didn't even see his second birthday, but Phoebe was always a comfort to her tiny buddy.

After Jerry passed, Joanne thought Phoebe needed another kitty companion with a disability. An adorable little tripod rescued by the staff at her congressman's office seemed like the perfect match. But the sweet, affectionate little boy kitten, named Veto, quickly turned into a feline Mafioso, and Phoebe's tranquil life turned into a nightmare. Veto bullied cats and people, yet he idolized the dogs. Everyone, even Joanne's vet, said she deserved a nicer kitty. Joanne felt guilty about Veto harassing Phoebe.

Her friends suggested getting the hyper kitten a puppy to distract his attention from Phoebe, so Joanne took in Charlotte, a tiny Toy Spaniel rescued in an SPCA hoarder raid. That also backfired, as Charlotte joined forces with Veto to torment Phoebe. She watched the Devil's Duo from above—her safe place—while they tore around the house. Veto couldn't climb well due to his missing rear leg and Charlotte the dog was earthbound, but somehow that spaniel could still steal Phoebe's food from spots the Afghans and disabled Veto couldn't reach. Phoebe began hiding more from the terrible twosome. Joanne tried to make it up to Phoebe by spending special private time with her.

Cats trick us into thinking they are immortal. They age more subtly than dogs. They don't gray around the muzzle and they stay agile much longer. Phoebe didn't look old at all. She was always dignified. Never a real fan of toys or playing, she just wanted to be loved, purring at top vibration. Joanne caught glimpses of her advancing years, like a speckling in one eye, and the gradual loss of muscle tone. Whenever a medical issue cropped up, Joanne took her to the vet.

After Phoebe turned twelve, Joanne noticed something wasn't quite right. Phoebe began to vomit. At first, Joanne didn't think anything of it. Phoebe's luxuriously long coat made hairballs just a fact of life. She started hiding more and eating less.

The diagnosis: irritable bowel syndrome. They put Phoebe on steroids, but she couldn't tolerate the medication well. She quickly went downhill.

Sometime in April, shortly after Phoebe came home from a procedure, she lost her rhinestone collar. Joanne didn't know exactly when it disappeared. Joanne searched in every one of Phoebe's favorite places, including under a vanity, the shelves of a linen closet, and inside a cedar closet. Phoebe remained collarless.

Then came the day Joanne had dreaded since Phoebe fell ill. Joanne left right after dismissal on the last day of school and immediately took her elderly cat to be put to sleep. She buried Phoebe without her collar, but with her favorite scratching post—the old running shoe.

That August, Joanne was going through a difficult time. She was looking for an item in her cedar closet when she spied something sparkly. Propped upon a pillow, as if someone carefully placed it there, was Phoebe's missing collar. The catch was securely fastened. Some stray strands of Phoebe's luxurious fur were wrapped around the rhinestones.

"Phoebe wanted me to find it when the time was right," Joanne said. "I keep it next to my computer so I can touch it, and maybe, just maybe, hear my Phoebe purr again."

*****

Joanne Anderson, a retired teacher, has written a weekly shelter rescue column in three Long Island newspapers for the past thirty-eight years. Initially the goal of writing the column was to coax readers into their municipal shelter to adopt the many overlooked cats and dogs, but it has blossomed into much more, including working in the Westminster Kennel Club press room.

Pumpkin

Pumpkin, a ginger kitten, was supposed to be a gift for Cari Flora's six-year-old son, Dakota. But as often happens with cats, the kitten chose his own person, and that happened to be Mom, Cari.

The name Pumpkin came from his obvious similarity to the popular Halloween jack-o-lantern, with his dark orange stripes. Unlike a real pumpkin, though, he had some belly and body spots. Sixteen-pound Pumpkin always slept with Cari and her hubby, Ric, usually between Cari's legs or at her feet.

He was sweet, playful and loved to cuddle! Cari described him as her "cuddle buddy." It didn't matter if Cari took a nap on a bed or a recliner, Pumpkin was always up for a good snuggle.

Pumpkin was a true predator—or as much of a predator as an indoor cat can be. He was a feared fly hunter. He'd take out anything that moved within his realm. Even on the bed, he could not resist the urge to hunt. He attacked that hidden prey under the bed covers whenever Cari moved her legs. Sometimes, when he felt particularly rambunctious, his needle teeth and claws penetrated, not only the comforter and the sheet, but a couple of layers of flesh too.

Then Pumpkin's world changed, and not for the better—at least from the orange tabby's perspective. Families are constantly transforming, and as a species that craves routine, cats aren't fans of change. They love predictability, and nothing disrupts your routine more than a crying baby. When Pumpkin turned four years old, Cari brought home a human baby, Liam. Pumpkin was not pleased. He never growled or hissed at Liam, but he certainly kept his distance.

One evening when Liam was a couple of weeks old, Pumpkin darted out the door. Cari had read that it was normal for cats to be upset by the arrival of a baby. Friends assured her he would be back. Still, she was worried. Cari put up flyers all over the neighborhood.

As her friends promised, a few days later he magically appeared on their porch. He was hungry and dirty. He appeared happy to be home, but it was two nights before he slept in his normal spot at the foot of her bed.

Several weeks later, Pumpkin snuck outside unnoticed. The flyers reappeared on street signs around the neighborhood. This time, he was gone for a week.

Another five months passed before he made his final escape. Nobody knows exactly what happened, but Cari believes, under darkness of night Pumpkin slipped out through the garage when Ric left for work. This time he didn't come back.

As before, they searched the neighborhood and covered every telephone pole they could find with flyers. Over the next few months, the family visited the animal shelters multiple times to check out the new arrivals. They monitored adopt-a-pet events hoping he'd show up as a cat in need of a home. Cari continued to drop off flyers at area vet clinics. She spoke to hundreds of people. Nobody had seen Pumpkin.

For months, Cari held out hope that he'd reappear in the garage, but he never did. When it was obvious their orange boy wasn't coming home, they adopted Misti, a year-old cat from a Craiglists ad. Once again, the new kitty favored Cari.

After a particularly stressful day, Cari tossed and turned in bed, but sleep evaded her. One of the cats jumped up on the bed by her feet. There was even a playful pounce and attack on Cari's moving feet. Not painful, but a weird sensation nevertheless—an oddly Pumpkin thing to do. Thinking it was Misti, Cari waited a few minutes for her to lie down, then reached down to pet her. There was nothing there. Misti wasn't even in the room.

"Um, okay," Cari thought.

Whoever had jumped on the bed moved around a bit and lay down between her legs, just as Pumpkin had always done. Once again, Cari reached around to pet the cat, knowing it had to be Misti. As before, there was no one to pet.

There, at her feet, a shadowy indention curled up on the comforter. Although Cari could see no visible kitty, the comforter moved in a steady pattern of inhaling and exhaling.

There was no doubt in her mind: That indention on the bed was Pumpkin. The grief, the loss, the pain—all the emotions she hoped were over—flooded back. This invisible presence confirmed what she'd already feared. Pumpkin was gone. He wouldn't be back, ever. It wasn't the ending she wanted, but at least she had closure. She also had comfort.

Cari patted the spot, and simply told him, "Goodnight." A few moments later, she felt Pumpkin jump down. Soon after, full-bodied Misti entered in the room, joining Cari on the bed.

Years later, Cari and her family made the first of several moves. This time, they took up residence in a new house in Pennsylvania, where they adopted a dog. Leap ahead three years. Cari's middle child, Euressa, who is now an adult, adopted an abandoned calico kitty with her boyfriend, Keifer. They named the cat Cookie.

As often happens with young families, tough times required the young couple to move in with Ric's parents. During the move, Cookie bolted out of the apartment. Despite extensive searches, they never found Cookie.

After the family regained their financial footing, Cari and Ric bought a home in Dover, Pennsylvania. Euressa, her family and Cookie's three kittens moved in with them. Since that time, Euressa has spied what she believes to be Cookie's ghost hanging out in the kitchen. Sometimes she catches Cookie dashing past her.

Cari, too, has experienced phantom kitties in the new house. One evening she had a headache, so she settled down for a nap. As she laid there, something light, like a small kitten, walked in a circle, patted the bed with its paws, then dropped to the mattress. It couldn't have been one of their living cats. They avoid Cari and Ric's room because the dog sleeps on the bedroom floor at night. The sensation of a jump onto the bed felt too light to be Pumpkin, or even Cookie.

Cari believes the kitten may have been a tiny kitten they rescued. When they took in four-week-old Ivy, he was very ill. Despite heroic efforts, the little guy didn't make it. Euressa still has his ashes.

Sometimes Cari sees a dark cat-shaped figure run across the room dashing up the stairs, and sometimes she watches an orange shape do the same. She suspects Pumpkin still drops in for an occasional visit.

*****

Cari Flora is mom to three humans and grandmom to one. She's also mom to three cats, two frogs, a dog, and a bearded dragon, and grandmom to four cats, three birds, and a dragon. They are just your average paranormal family.

Furrdy

As a thirteen-year-old in the early 1970s, Jynjyr was in bed with the flu when her late grandmother checked on her. During her life, Nana had been a nurse. Jynjyr's body ached; she felt lousy all over. The teenager needed a little TLC in the middle of the night. As she lay in bed trying to fall back to sleep, she felt a cool hand press against her forehead. Someone was doing a quick temperature check. The hand was too small to be her dad's and she knew it wasn't her mom. In fact, there was not a living soul in the room. Jynjyr froze, unable to move or even open her eyes. "It scared the crap out of me," she recalls.

In her next encounter at the age of sixteen, she heard the clicking of toenails against the floor. It had to be her dog, Duke, who had recently died.

Life moved on. Jynjyr went to college, then moved out on her own finding work as a mechanical engineer. Her job entailed making precision metal cutting tools used in the manufacture of car and airplane parts.

In spring 1991, a six-month-old stray kitten showed up at a friend's house while Jynjyr was visiting. The poor thing had been hanging around the neighborhood. Judging by his friendliness with people, Jynjyr suspected he'd been a pet who got lost or had been left behind like yesterday's trash. Jynjyr felt sorry for the shorthaired boy with a fluffy tail.

When she picked him up, the silver tabby and white kitten shed fur all over her. He immediately burst into the most endearing purr. That was all she needed. She named him Furrdy, and he moved in with Jynjyr and her two-year-old rescue cat, Whiskers. The three of them spent the next sixteen years together.

Within a week, he was sleeping next to her head on the pillow. She figured Furrdy staked out the area next to her head because Whiskers always curled up against her hip or between her thighs.

Jynjyr couldn't help spoiling him. As a stray, Furrdy must have struggled to find food. As a kept kitty, he loved to eat, especially his tasty treats. Even after he got used to having several square meals every day, he proved to be an unapologetic foodie.

After watching Jynjyr get the goody dispenser from the cabinet the first time, he knew exactly where she kept them. He just needed opposable thumbs. Although he couldn't pull the cabinet door open himself, he wasn't shy about reminding her when it was snack time. At ten o'clock, the appointed time for treats, he sat by the special cabinet and started smacking at the door—a very loud request for his delicacy. In the morning, he'd wake Jynjyr up demanding his breakfast. Furrdy got older and heavier. Before long, the skinny kitten transformed into a chubby chonker. He peaked at eighteen pounds.

In 2000, about the time Jynjyr moved into her current house, she purchased a bigger bed. With the arrival of the larger sleeping space, XL-sized Furrdy chose a new sleeping spot. His new bedtime routine involved jumping up on the foot of the bed, walking a few steps to snuggle against her hips or lie down on her ankles. Regardless of where he slept, once he was settled, Jynjyr couldn't move.

In 2006, Furrdy suddenly dropped weight and Jynjyr noticed he was drooling. She immediately rushed him to the vet. He had oral cancer. His hard-to-see tumor was so advanced, the vet recommended letting him go on the spot. Jynjyr wasn't prepared at all to say goodbye. Furrdy was the first pet she'd ever had to put to sleep. She called a friend to come to the clinic to be with her. Furrdy was cremated and his ashes placed in a little metal urn.

After sixteen years together, the house wasn't the same without her XL-sized buddy. Bedtime certainly had something missing. Jynjyr still had Whiskers, who was well into her eighteenth year. However, Whiskers, who with his achy joints couldn't manage the two-foot leap to the mattress, had stopped sleeping on the bed. Without Furrdy, Jynjyr slept alone.

A month later, Jynjyr lay in bed half-awake, resting on her side, when she felt the plop of a heavy cat landing on the foot of the bed. Something substantial settled on her ankles. She immediately looked at her feet, but there was nothing there. By that time, the sensation on her ankles ceased.

The heavy animal who jumped up on her bed couldn't have been dainty, nine-pound Whiskers, who *always* curled up on Jynjyr's belly or at her legs. It had to be Furrdy.

Was she dreaming or did something remarkable just happen? She had felt that bulky body jump on the bed for more than a decade-and-a-half. She knew how it felt when he landed on the bed.

His brief presence brought back the pain and second-guessing, the what-ifs, woulda, coulda, shouldas. She got weepy. "I wondered if I hadn't tried to look, would he have stayed longer?" she said. Jynjyr thinks Furrdy just wanted one last snuggle and to say goodbye.

Several weeks later, Furrdy returned. Around the same time of night, Jynjyr felt the mattress move as that same weight landed on the bed. This time she didn't feel the bulk on her ankles, only the tremendous bounce of the mattress. She didn't bother to look. But as with the earlier visit, he was there and then he wasn't. More time had passed since she lost Furrdy, so she wasn't as sad. "It wasn't quite so fresh in my mind," she said. "I'm almost nostalgic about it. He came back for just one more, 'Hey, hi. Bye.'"

Jynjyr knew what she felt, but once again wondered, did it really happen or was she dreaming?

Later on, Jynjyr experienced two more visits, but they were so fleeting—the weight of a cat landing on the bed but nothing there.

A couple of years after Furrdy's return, Jynjyr started attending media conventions—gatherings of television and movie fans. At one event, she struck up a conversation with an amateur ghost hunter. When Jynjyr told the woman about her experiences with Furrdy, the ghost hunter assured her it was not unusual for a well-loved companion animal to visit. Following that conversation, Jynjyr acknowledges her own paranormal experience as well as those of others.

Over the twenty years she's lived in her current house, she has lost five cats, but she hasn't been visited by anyone but Furrdy. She wishes some of her other cats would drop by too.

*****

Jynjyr is cat mom to three feline "children." She is just trying to survive the COVID pandemic and get back to having fun during the summer.

Disco Cat

Coral Cashes had gone through a rough patch in her life, including ending a long-term relationship. The loss of someone to share expenses meant she had to work long hours just to get by. With more time away from home, Coral knew that Isis, her French bulldog named after the Egyptian goddess, would be lonely. With Isis' second birthday fast approaching, Coral decided she would give the dog a cat.

For several months, she visited the cats at the local animal shelter, but she didn't find a kitty with the right temperament. Finally, she found an adorable four-month-old gray and white tuxedo kitten with bright yellow eyes. Coral named her Disco.

Isis greeted her new companion with curiosity. She approached the kitten slowly—ears perked, eyes wide. Adventurous and trusting, the kitten allowed the dog's advances. After giving each other a good sniff, they immediately started playing. As Coral had hoped, the odd couple became inseparable. Wherever Coral found Isis, she found Disco—often cuddling or grooming each other. They seldom left the other's side.

When Disco turned two, Coral gave her a collar with a bell. During the course of a normal day, the bell jingled as the active kitty dashed through the house, scratched herself, or jumped on counters.

One night, Disco escaped from the house. In the darkness, she hid beneath some bushes, too scared to show herself. Fortunately, the bell on her collar gave her away, leading Coral to her hiding spot. After that, Coral made sure Disco's collar always had a bell.

The two buddies grew old together, but in 2011 Isis developed a stomach cancer. Goodbye is always hard, especially when Isis was only nine. Afterward, Disco, who was seven at the time, grew closer to Coral, never leaving her side. Coral continued to replace Disco's collars as they became lost or worn.

During Disco's life, Coral moved a lot. When Disco was thirteen, Coral's home burned to the ground. For three years, they lived in a condo with the perfect kitty entertainment center: a window with a front row seat to Lake Minnie. Through her view to the world, Disco watched bugs fluttering around and birds landing on tree branches just out of reach. Every night, Disco jumped up on Coral's bed and slept by her human's feet.

Jump forward to 2020, the year nobody wants to relive. In January, after Coral's friend Sandy split up with the father of her infant. Coral and Disco hurriedly moved in to help out. The move wasn't all bad for Disco. The apartment had perfect kitty windows with a view of Lake Frederica, a beautiful body of water. Just like the old days, Disco laid in front of the windows bird-watching. It was her favorite way to the pass time.

Cats don't handle stress well. It can unleash illnesses their little bodies have been harboring for months, possibly years. Two weeks after they moved in, Disco went from fairly healthy to death's door, a victim of sudden kidney failure. Coral tried to keep her clean, but poor Disco vomited so frequently her coat took on the same acrid odor. The day after Valentine's Day, it was time to say goodbye. To keep her as comfortable as possible and minimize her anxiety, Coral arranged for a vet to come to the house. Sixteen-year-old Disco took her last breath on her favorite blanket, surrounded by people who loved her, gazing out the floor-to-ceiling windows overlooking the trees. Disco wore a leopard print collar with a purple bell and a purple heart-shaped nametag.

Coral was surprised by her reaction to Disco's passing. She expected more pain, more anguish. Instead, Coral felt as if her beloved cat was still with her.

A week later, Coral got engaged to Zack.

Soon, Coral, Sandy, and Zack, could hear tiny cat footsteps padding across the laminate floor, as if Disco was still prancing around the house. Occasionally, they would catch a momentary whiff of cat puke—the same smell as Disco and her bed after her health failed. At first, Coral dismissed the faint stench as just mind tricks. She washed everything Disco had come in contact with, but even after all the washing and scrubbing, they could still occasionally detect cat puke.

GHOST CATS 2

In June 2020, because of the COVID-19 quarantine and other circumstances, Coral moved out of Sandy's apartment by the lake and in with her fiancé, Zack, along with his fourteen-year-old cat, Leon. Coral found herself suddenly overwhelmed with grief. Now her loss of Disco felt fresh and raw, and much more intense than she experienced immediately after his death.

A few months later, Sandy shared a weird event. The babysitter had put Sandy's nineteen-month-old son, Matthew, to bed, when she heard a little bell ringing. It sounded like the bell on a cat collar. She knew Sandy didn't have a cat, so the only logical explanation was that the baby was making the noise. She checked the nursery to make sure he wasn't playing with a toy left in the crib, but Matthew was fast asleep. The sitter returned to the couch. Again, she heard the bell, but this time, it sounded closer. Suddenly, she felt a cat rub against her leg. She looked down, but there was no cat.

When Sandy returned home, the sitter told her what happened. Sandy immediately thought about Disco, who always wore a bell on her collar.

After learning about the sitter's weird experience, Coral suddenly understood why she hadn't grieved when Disco first died, but came apart when she left the apartment. After Disco's euthanasia, she may have awakened next to her window, not realizing she had passed on. Disco was still at Sandy's. When Coral moved away, Disco stayed behind. Coral had lost her kitty for good—or so she thought.

One day, Coral dropped by Sandy's apartment to pick up the last of her things, to retrieve her mail, and catch up on gossip. After her visit, unexplained things began to occur at Zack's apartment. Every now and then during the day, Coral caught the scent of cat puke, and some nights, as the couple was lying in bed, Zack felt a cat crawling on him—not unusual, except Leon wasn't in the bedroom.

Since Disco in her disembodied form moved back with Coral, Sandy reports she no longer hears or smells Disco at her place. Coral believes that when Disco saw her again at Sandy's, she followed her to the new apartment. Coral is happy and relieved that Disco joined her. "Knowing she's with me again gives me peace," she said.

*****

Coral Cashes is a wife, mother, twin sister, Floridian, artist, and animal lover.

Larry the Cat

Linda Reinhold had two roommates in her college dorm—one with a body temperature of 98.6 degrees and another with no temperature at all. The ghost in her dorm room liked to hide stuff, especially Linda's hairbrush. It also turned the radio on and off and knocked things over. So, Linda knew the feel of a haunted home.

The Crystal Lake, Illinois, house she and hubby Bill bought in August of 1999 was not paranormally occupied, at least not at the time. They moved in with their two kids, Leanna and Michael, ages eleven and seven, and two fourteen-year-old cats, Felix and Larry.

Not long after they moved in, Felix, the friendlier, more outgoing cat, passed away. Larry, the remaining cat, was a white shorthaired kitty with large patches of dark gray with black stripes. Larry always loved Bill, but never warmed up to anyone else. In Felix's absence, though, Larry transformed into a friendly, affectionate kitty. He typically slept at the foot of the bed between Bill and Linda's ankles, but sometimes he'd share nighttime snuggles with the kids too.

In spring of 2001, Linda noticed that Larry had suddenly started snoring. The vet delivered the devastating news: Larry had a malignant nasal tumor. Then came worse news: Surgery was prohibitively expensive. Even if they could afford it, there was no guarantee Larry would live longer or that it would improve his quality of life. The Reinholds elected to forgo intervention, keeping Larry comfortable and letting him live out his life, which at sixteen had been a long and happy one. When the time came, the family took him to the veterinarian and said their tearful goodbyes.

Almost a year after Larry's passing, the family felt ready to love a cat again. They adopted two kittens, Milo and Sammy, from the local shelter.

It was only after the kittens were fully grown that strange things began to happen in the Reinhold home. One night, Linda and Leanna were sitting on the edge of Linda's bed watching a ghost hunter TV show. Sometime earlier, while Bill enjoyed a bowl of ice cream in the bed, he accidentally dropped a wadded paper towel on the floor. As

GHOST CATS 2

Linda and Leanna followed the ghost action on television, they both saw the paper towel ball roll over on its own. They looked at each other. Wide-eyed, Leanna asked, "Did you see that?!" Linda had seen it. Leanna ran downstairs and got her dad.

Bill inspected the room for anything that could have caused a breeze. The heat wasn't on—no air flowed from the vent. The windows were securely shut. No one could find an obvious explanation for the paper towel moving on its own.

The next day, after folding laundry in the family room, Linda sat cross-legged on the floor looking through the DVD library on the entertainment center shelf. In Linda's peripheral vision, positioned next to her knee she saw a balled-up sock suddenly roll over by itself.

She stared at the sock and smiled. "There's a little spirit moving things here. What could it be?"

She thought about what the two experiences had in common—ball-shaped objects on the floor moved. What's on the floor? A cat. It had to be Larry!

Linda told everyone, "I think we have a little ghost in the house." Although everyone suspected the little ghost cat was Larry, the Reinholds had no way to confirm it until guests described their own encounters with the ghost cat.

Not long after the Great Sock Incident, Linda was sitting with fifteen-year-old Leanna and her friend Sandra in Leanna's bedroom when Sandra looked up and said, "You have a ghost cat. I just saw him." Sandra described a dark gray and white cat who had just jumped on the bed and vanished. "It's Larry!" Linda and Leanna exclaimed. They finally had their confirmation.

Larry was also seen on two other occasions, weeks apart, by two of Michael's friends. The boys described almost identical encounters with Larry. Both kids saw a gray and white cat walking down the hall. When they reached out to pet him, the cat disappeared.

On another night, Linda felt the soft thump of a cat jumping on the bed, followed by the sensation of paws walking a few steps before settling down in Larry's traditional sleeping spot. The pressure against her ankles felt perfectly normal. She looked at her feet to see whether Milo or Sammy had joined them. The moon was bright that night and moonlight flowed into the room. She could make out the sleeping form of Bill next to her. However, there was no cat to be seen. Reaching down, her fingers found dead air. Immediately, the pressure against her feet vanished.

When she shared her experience with Bill and the kids, she

learned Larry was an equal opportunity haunter. Although no one in the family actually saw Larry, everyone had received bedtime visits from the ghost cat.

For the next two years, Larry continued to visit them sporadically. Sometimes he'd sleep with them every night for a week, then he failed to show up for weeks at a time. Gradually, the time between visits grew longer and longer, until one day Linda couldn't remember the last time she'd felt his presence. Somehow she knew Larry had finally left for his next adventure.

"I believe ghosts hang around places they loved in life. I'd like to think his sweet spirit is romping in fresh fields with his pal, Felix, perhaps with all of the cats we have loved and lost, somewhere in the Great Beyond."

*****

Linda Lessmann Reinhold, who graduated Stephens College in Columbia, Missouri, with a bachelor's degree in fine arts, has worked as a colorist for Marvel Comics and First Comics. She is cofounder of The Gorblimey Press, and has worked as an inking assistant to her husband, Bill Reinhold. You can see their work at www.deviantart.com/billreinhold.

Pavel

Mindy loves anything that's rare and exotic. As an antiques dealer and *Star Trek* collector in Alabama, she always got the chance to take home the most exotic of her finds. Over the years, she built up quite a collection of antique jewelry, illuminated books, and original series *Star Trek* memorabilia. In her mind, though, all her collections paled compared to the elegant blue-gray coat of a dirty gray kitten she found abandoned next to a dumpster at a nearby antiques mall. She picked up the pathetic kitten and took him home.

Mindy immediately bonded with him. He may not have had a pedigree, but Mindy had no doubt that silvery waif had Russian Blue somewhere in his family tree. She named him Pavel, after the

Russian Ensign Chekov, the *U.S.S. Enterprise's* navigation officer. Like pedigreed Russian Blues, Pavel the kitten was reserved, observing situations before jumping in.

Mindy already had a six-year-old black cat named Scotty, after *Enterprise's* chief engineer. With slow introductions, the two felines bonded, becoming life-long buddies. Scotty, the patient older brother, mostly tolerated the rambunctious kitten who used his back haunches as a launching pad.

After Pavel matured, the solid gray and solid black cats looked like photocopies of each other, with Pavel's copy looking as if it was running low on black toner.

Pavel always started the morning with polite meows on important topics—mostly reminding Mindy she had yet fed him. He only meowed once or twice, but he sat by his food bowl until she got the memo.

On those days when she worked at home, researching new memorabilia acquisitions, Pavel slept in an oval cat bed on the corner of her computer desk. He'd wake up and plow through her collection on his way to the kitchen to check his bowl.

The year Pavel turned eight, his health declined. He suffered from frequent bouts of pancreatitis. For two years, he was in and out of the animal hospital. They placed him on pain medications, antibiotics and subcutaneous fluids. He often accompanied Mindy to work, so she could feed him every couple of hours.

One morning as Mindy was preparing for work, she realized he wasn't sitting by the bowl waiting for her. She found him laying motionless on his side in his bed on her desk. A smoke-colored orb hovered above him. Appropriately, the glowing orb reminded Mindy of a cheesy *Star Trek* (original series, of course) special effects. Tears flowed as she dug a hole in the backyard.

Later that day, as she opened a can of cat food for Scotty, Mindy spotted another glowing gray orb in her kitchen suspended over the Pavel's food bowl. It precisely matched the shade of slate gray in Pavel's coat. The luminous globe looked as if someone had somehow filled a soap bubble with cigarette smoke. She looked directly at it, and it popped. It had to be Pavel, waiting for his dinner. She brushed a tear and spooned a dollop of pâté into his dish. She checked it later, hopeful. It had been eaten, but she knew Scotty was the one who ate it.

Moving from behind her, the sphere bobbed up and down as it floated past her. It disappeared when it came in contact with the door that led from the kitchen to the garage. The whole episode lasted only a few seconds.

Weeks later, Mindy sat on the living room floor looking through her latest estate sale acquisition. Scotty lay on the carpet next to her, occasionally stretching and jumbling Mindy's carefully organized piles of books and figurines. Out of the corner of her eye, a cat-sized smoky gray shadow ran from out of the eastern wall of the room. It had the same exact build as Pavel. It *was* Pavel.

Scotty knew it too. He turned his head, tracking as it moved across the room. The orb playfully pounced in the middle of the memorabilia pile, moving nothing, then drifted on. For an instant, it was so close Mindy could have touched it—she wanted to, but she didn't. It moved across the room and faded into the wall shared by her office.

Mindy left the collection on the floor and checked the office. Over Pavel's favorite cat bed hovered the smoky orb. In a flash, it vanished.

Mindy believes Pavel returned for the same reason that humans return to their loved ones: to show her that he had shed his painful old body. He was forever in his prime. "The spirit who ran through the living room was happy and healthy again. I treasure the healthy, happy, and mischievous cat being my last image of him. Not the weak kitty who left this world. I miss him terribly, but I'm happy that he's happy," she said.

Unfortunately, she hasn't seen him since, and nobody else has had the pleasure of experiencing Pavel since he visited Mindy and Scotty.

The Feline Phantom

Praline the Persian cat was quite the celebrity in her day. When Praline turned twelve, her human mom, Paula Gregg of Lexington, South Carolina, began writing a blog. In those early days of cat blogs, Praline's two-thousand-plus social media fans knew her as the Diva of the Cat Blogosphere.

Praline had enormous green eyes and a full set of seal point markings, including a seal-colored mask that covered two-thirds of her face. The remaining third was adorned with dilute tortoiseshell markings. The distinctive markings gave her an uncanny resemblance to the Phantom in *Phantom of the Opera*. Paula liked to call Praline her Phantom Cat. The kitty with a perpetual Persian scowl was perfect for Internet stardom, and cat-craving web surfers couldn't get enough of her.

Miss Paula's Sweet Praline (the name on her pedigree) came to live with Paula when she was twelve weeks old, while Paula was going through a divorce after twenty-one years of marriage. Over the years, the Phantom kitty saw her human through numerous other traumas, including being fired from her first job and changing careers. Paula then trudged the rigorous road to earning her PhD, adjusting to her first position as a college professor, then becoming the education program manager for the State of South Carolina. That's a lot of stress. Paula's clinical depression and thirteen surgeries over five years only exacerbated her emotional health.

Through it all, Praline purred by her side. For almost sixteen years, Praline was the perfect therapist as Paula struggled through trauma after trauma. Praline was Paula's heart kitty.

At home, Paula spent much of her time in a large, open room she called the great room. When Paula watched TV in that space, Praline often sat across the room, her paws primly posed together, staring at Paula with those wide Persian eyes.

Paula spent the rest of her time in her office in the back of the house, working at her desk, where she pounded out her dissertation, and later, college lesson plans. Eventually, through Paula, Praline wrote her famous blog posts in that office.

At four-foot-eleven, Paula was too short to reach both the floor and the keyboard at the same time, so she stabilized her feet on a footstool she kept under the desk. Often, Paula's feet had to share her stool with Praline, from where the Persian supervised and monitored Paula's progress. Praline's tail brushed across her legs so frequently, Paula no longer noticed the Phantom Cat's attempt to hog the stool.

Eventually, Praline's fourteen years caught up with her. Paula noticed a white bump beside her nose. The vet removed the lump and diagnosed it as a benign mast cell tumor. Great! Paula believed her feline soul mate would be fine.

A year after the surgery, things went south; this time another tumor developed that wasn't benign. Paula realized Praline was very sick when the once-luxurious tortoiseshell fur looked greasy and clumpy. Even her thick coat couldn't hide Praline's protruding bones.

The vet was confounded. The blood work showed she was fine. She prescribed medication to increase Praline's appetite and something to control nausea. Paula coaxed Praline to eat, hand feeding her a morsel at a time. In March 2011 the veterinarian found a cancerous mass in Praline's digestive tract. She offered a number of treatment options, but Paula decided rather than putting Praline through the invasive diagnostics and the trauma of treatment, they would manage her pain and provide a quality life for as long as possible. Paula did everything she could to keep Praline comfortable over the next month; then the downhill slide swelled to an avalanche.

In late April, the vet asked Paula if she was ready to let Praline go. Paula wasn't. She had envisioned a fairy tale ending: the beautiful princess kitty holding court at home with her loved one by her side slipping naturally into permanent sleep.

The vet still saw some fight in those huge eyes, but warned Paula she would probably be back within a week for the final time. The next day, Praline stopped eating, and, for the first time ever, she refused even her favorite treats. Paula got the message. Her time with Praline had drawn to a close. Paula told her Phantom she was going to a place where she would no longer be in pain. Just five months before Praline turned sixteen, Paula helped her cross the Rainbow Bridge. From the day she was diagnosed with cancer to her last, only one month had passed.

Praline's pain may have stopped, but Paula's had just begun. Without Praline to keep her company, Paula felt so alone and isolated. Her Phantom had left a Praline-shaped hole in Paula's heart. She knew there would be other cats in her life someday, but at that moment, Paula was drowning in a deep well of depression and loneliness. On a good day, Paula only broke into tears once or twice.

Three months later, Paula received an email with photos of a pair of kittens she had decided to buy when they were old enough. Until they arrived, Paula had to endure more long, lonely nights. Shortly after the Fourth of July, Paula sat on her chair at her computer, staring at the photos. Tears streamed down her cheeks. Her loneliness seemed intensified by what seemed the far-off arrival of her new kittens. She felt so terribly alone.

Paula went to her great room to watch TV and sat in the recliner she had shared with Praline. She glanced toward the foyer beside the glass curio cabinet where she kept her reminders of Praline: the urn containing her ashes, a photo, her favorite toy, and a lock of her fur. There in the foyer, next to the curio cabinet, sat Praline, paws primly posed together, staring at her human as she had done so often in life. Paula immediately turned her head back to focus on the vision, but Praline had vanished.

At first Paula was very skeptical. She was trained as a mathematician and embraced logical reasoning. "I was skeptical about the paranormal, at first," she said. But Paula's heart knew Praline had paid her a brief visit. She may have suffered from depression, but she certainly had never seen hallucinations before. Still, she didn't tell anyone else about her experience, fearing no one would believe her.

"I wish she had stayed longer," Paula said. "One would think this would upset me more, but her appearance brought me comfort. I believe she was telling me it would be okay and she was still with me. In that darkest moment, when I needed her most, she appeared."

That was the last time Paula *saw* her Phantom, but Praline didn't abandon her human.

Not long after Praline's hallway appearance, Paula was posting on social media at her office computer desk. Still grieving, she felt isolated and alone. As always, she steadied her feet on her footstool. Once again, she experienced something unexpected, yet so familiar— the pleasant, feathery sensation of soft fur brushing across her legs. It only lasted a few seconds, but the brief encounter provided her with relief and comfort. Paula instantly relaxed.

Praline dropped by for two more under-the-desk visits before Paula's new kittens, Truffle and Brulee, arrived in September. All of Praline's appearances occurred when Paula's depression was most intense.

After the kittens became official residents, Praline's visits ceased. Brulee and Truffle turned out to be capable therapists, at least for day-to-day stress.

One animal communicator told Paula that Praline sometimes stopped by incognito, but she didn't make herself known because she wanted Truffle and Brulee to look after Paula.

It had been many years since Praline's last known visit, and Paula believed her time with her Phantom companion was over. But in 2020, the year nobody wants to relive, Paula's stress grew out of control as her already-complicated life became even more arduous.

In late 2019/early 2020 Paula was struck down by an illness, which her doctor later suspected was COVID-19. (It took eighteen months for Paula to breathe normally.)

Her mother's Alzheimer's disease had progressed significantly. Paula was elected president of the Cat Writers' Association, which increased her responsibility and her workload. And the coup de grâce was Brulee and Truffle both battled life-threatening illnesses. Within a two-and-a-half-month period, Truffle almost died of bladder stones and suffered from major infections and high pH levels. Brulee had a bad reaction to an FVRCP injection that kept her in the emergency animal hospital for four nights.

When the going gets tough, you need the best. Praline came on her own. One night, Brulee and Truffle were both recovering at home. After Paula laid down to go to sleep, she felt the slight bounce of a cat jumping on the bed. Paula glanced down to see who was wishing her good night. To her surprise, she found neither Truffle nor Brulee. It had to be Praline. Paula sat up and said, "Hello, Praline. Thank you for coming to visit me." She slipped off to sleep, finally welcoming a peaceful night.

A few months later, Paula was trying to sleep when she felt a pounce on the bed and a cat walking beside her legs. She looked. This time, on the other side of the bed, she found Brulee and Truffle curled up, sleeping so soundly it couldn't have been either of them. At the source of the movement, she found no cat. The little Phantom had made herself known again.

Paula believed Praline dropped by because she picked up on Paula's stress about how out-of-control the entire world felt. As always, Praline's simple presence brought Paula peace.

Since then, Praline visited a few more times. She made herself known ten times over the past nine years, at the very moments Paula most needed her.

"She appears during times of emotional or physical stress," Paula said. "She's letting me know it's going to be okay. From the beginning, Praline's mere presence calmed me. She still does.

"I'm a control freak and my mind races throughout the day. I've been told I'm most receptive before I go to sleep. That's when she visits. Praline made a believer out of me. She was my heart kitty, and this proves it. She's letting me know she's still with me. She always brings me comfort."

*****

Paula Gregg, Ph.D., was an award-winning blogger and photographer for Sweet Purrfections where she wrote about Persian cat health, daily care, education, and the human-animal bond. Paula passed away in May, 2022 after a short fight with pancreatic cancer. At the time, she was the president of the Cat Writers' Association.

The Spy Who Loved Me

Rhonda Barrientos, a long-time cat rescuer in North Texas, and her husband, Andy, have been married for more than thirty-five years. For the first seven years, they had no children, so they focused their nurturing instincts on their dog and two cats.

In 1990, Rhonda spotted a newspaper ad for a pair of six-week-old Russian Blue kittens. The breeder was a motivated seller because this litter was unplanned. Rhonda already had two cats and certainly didn't need any more. But she'd always adored Russian Blues, so this was her chance get one without having to take out a mortgage.

As she sat on the floor at the woman's house, the little male kitten stole Rhonda's heart. Across the room, Andy was falling hard for his sister. They couldn't make a decision, so they left with both kittens.

What do you call a pair of Russian Blue kittens? Boris and Natasha, of course—after the Russian spies in *The Adventures of Rocky and Bullwinkle.*

The fine-boned Boris tipped the scales at just ten pounds at his peak. Rhonda couldn't resist his brilliant green eyes and lavender paw pads. Like many Blues, he was quite the conversationalist. Whenever Rhonda or Andy arrived home, he greeted them at the door with an emphatic hello. He held most of his conversations at mealtime. Impatient, he hounded Rhonda, "Hurry up opening that can, already!" She didn't have to be in the same room to know who was vocalizing; she recognized his meow with her eyes closed—a distinctively male voice, softer and deeper than the other cats with a bit of a Texas twang. Every meow sounded like a question—with the pitch rising higher at the end of the sentence.

Finally, Rhonda gave birth to their first human baby. And on the momentous occasion of bringing Dylan home from the hospital, Boris greeted him with open paws. Boris adored Dylan from the moment their eyes met. He stood vigil by the infant's side whenever he could. The new parents struggled to keep Boris out of Dylan's crib, so they had to remember to close the door as they left the nursery.

Whenever Dylan cried, Boris always assumed the cat nearest to the baby was responsible for his distress. He ran over and smacked the unfortunate bystander. To comfort Dylan, Boris rubbed his forehead on Dylan's face; he would do anything in his power to get the baby to stop crying.

As the Barrientos family grew, they moved to a more accommodating home in nearby Irving, Texas. One of Boris's primary jobs was to visit anyone using the toilet and keep them company during the process.

The new house was like Heaven to elderly Boris. Several established pecan trees shaded the fenced backyard, with enough sunlight filtering through to satisfy the flower bed filled with purple irises. Before they moved in, the yard had been covered with lush Bermuda grass, but with the exception of a few isolated grass patches, the dogs wore most of it down until the yard resembled the surface of the moon.

Every now and then, Rhonda took Boris for supervised strolls around the yard. Until they moved, Boris' only taste of the outside had been through the kitchen windows. He took his time exploring, locating the grassy stretches and rubbing his face on the soft, fluffy sod. He couldn't resist stealing a nibble or two. Bermuda grass was the best!

In his early twenties Boris' health begin to decline—very gradually. He began to lose muscle tone and took on that rumpled old man look. He stopped grooming and started sleeping most of the day. His appetite waned. His bones protruded through his unkempt fur. Rhonda began brushing him regularly. He was a cooperative patient. He willingly took pills and accepted syringe dining.

One day Andy realized Boris needed some joy in his life. The poor old guy was too weak and feeble to visit his beloved yard any longer, so Andy planted some cat grass in a pot and brought it inside for him to enjoy. Boris's eyes lit up and he rubbed his face against it, just as he did in his younger years.

As he neared the end of his life, Boris began to feel cool to the touch. Rhonda set up a little sanctuary in the back bathroom with a comfy heated bed. He slept sequestered at night so the other cats wouldn't bother him or push him off his warm refuge.

One day, twenty-four-year-old Boris fell sleep on his heated bed and never woke up. They buried him in his beloved backyard, just outside Dylan's bedroom window. An angel statue marked his final resting spot.

Within a week of Boris's passing, Rhonda was in the house alone. She stopped in the front bathroom and left the door ajar. While she was sitting on the porcelain throne, she heard Boris' distinctive meow just outside the door.

She looked around. There were no kitties anywhere. They were all hanging out in the living room. "Right after you lose someone, there are parts of your brain that forget he's not with you any longer," Rhonda said. "For a moment I thought he was still alive, but I remembered, 'Oh, yeah. He's gone.'"

She dismissed it as her imagination or wishful thinking. "I just thought I hadn't accepted his death yet." But that was just the beginning of Boris' short communications campaign.

The next day, Rhonda and sixteen-year-old Dylan sat in the living room watching television, surrounded by their surviving kitties. Suddenly, above the TV, she heard a soft, deep cat meow, definitely Boris' voice. Immediately, she thought, "I know that voice."

As both she and Dylan turned simultaneously to look for the source of the sound, Dylan asked, "Did I just hear Boris?"

Then, out of Rhonda's peripheral vision, where the living room and hallway meet (outside the bathroom), she saw a cat-shaped disruption of the light. It reminded her of the cloaking effect from the movie *Predator*, or the Romulan/Klingon cloaking device from the original *Star Trek* movies. The outline even appeared to have a willowy tail. When she stared at it straight on, it appeared to rub against the corner of the wall and then moved into the kitchen. It lasted only a few seconds. Rhonda got up to check the hall, but found no cats hanging out there; they were all lounging in the living room.

Even though both Rhonda and Dylan heard it, none of the living room cats even lifted their heads to investigate.

A few days later, as Rhonda stood at the kitchen sink washing dishes, she felt a cat rub against her leg. She looked down, expecting to see one of her black kitties, but there was no visible cat. In a fraction of a second, the sensation vanished. It was over. "That was weird," she thought.

Over the next few weeks, Rhonda saw the shimmer and heard Boris' voice a few more times.

Boris' final contact with the Barrientos family came when Dylan had a dream that felt so real, he thought it was actually happening. In the dream, he woke up to the sound of Boris meowing at him. He and his mom were sitting at their antique dinner table, a table with legs the old kitty had face-marked for almost two and a half decades. On the table lounging casually on his side, Boris eyed them. Even in the dream, Dylan knew Boris had died, but he was back. He looked the same as the day he passed, a little bony and old, but still healthy and happy. Dylan and Rhonda lavished attention on the old kitty, petting him and talking to him. But all too soon, Boris jumped onto the floor and walked over to the French doors. He strolled through the glass as if it wasn't there. For a brief moment, Boris looked back as if saying goodbye and then went into the yard. Dylan followed him outside, but Boris had already moved on. Dylan suddenly awoke, but knew Boris was happy and free. That was the last contact Boris had with his beloved family.

"He didn't want to leave us," Dylan said. "I realize he couldn't stay forever." He felt sad that Boris had left for good. He wasn't ready to let his buddy go. Dylan said it was touching that he was the one Boris said his final goodbye to.

Rhonda believes, "He died when it was his time, but lingered long enough to let us know he was okay. Then he moved on to where dead kitties go. I think he had a strong desire to let us know he was still with us in a way."

Shadow Cat

Debbie De Louise had lost several cats over the last two decades. It was hard saying goodbye to every one of them, but there was a special sadness about Oliver, an elderly Siamese-mix with light-shaded color points. He had originally belonged to Debbie's mother, Florence, who adored kitties. When Florence's dementia advanced, and she moved to a nursing home, Debbie took Oliver.

Oliver adjusted to his new environment well. In Florence's absence, he grew very close to Debbie. Eventually, his age caught up with him. He passed away at seventeen of kidney failure. Debbie had him cremated and placed his ashes in an urn she kept in her bedroom.

Even with her other cat, the house felt wrong without him. She missed his dynamic blue eyes when she set out their dinner. She expected to see him on the couch, but of course, he wasn't there.

The Monday after Oliver's passing, Debbie took part in the weekly Rainbow Bridge candle-lighting ceremony online.[5] At the appointed time, soft music streamed from the computer speakers and the emcee read the names of the pets who had passed. When he spoke Oliver's name, Debbie lit his candle. She cried, but as the flame rose from the wick, she felt a release of the guilt and pain and anger and all those emotions that accompany losing someone you love.

In that moment, she felt lighter. Her feelings moved forward toward acceptance. She would always miss him, but she could look beyond the pain to recall all those joyful moments they experienced together.

Late the next afternoon, beams of sunlight streamed through the sliding glass patio door. Debbie sat at her computer in the living room working on an upcoming project when a rainbow appeared on the wall next to her, dancing against the white background.

It couldn't be an accident. It was a sign from Oliver. Over the decades she had sat at that exact spot at the same time of day under all different weather and light conditions, and never did a rainbow appear—not before that day or since. But the day after the Rainbow Bridge ceremony, that glowing spectrum of colors materialized just for Debbie. It shone brightly for about fifteen minutes, then began to fade until the late afternoon shadows replaced it.

"He knew I was thinking about him," Debbie said. "He wanted to make me feel better. He was trying to communicate that he was okay. He was on the Rainbow Bridge or in Heaven."

Debbie visited her mother often. Watching her mom's mental decline was hard enough, but knowing that Florence's soul mate had already passed made the visits almost unbearable. Florence never knew Oliver had preceded her in death. Debbie simply couldn't bring herself to tell her. Just eight months later, Florence joined him.

The following February, Debbie awoke and lay in her bed thinking

---

[5] https://www.rainbowsbridge.com

about the upcoming day. It was Florence's birthday—the first birthday since her passing.

It was early dawn, and the faintest blush of pink light seeped through Debbie's bedroom window. As she stared up, she felt a presence. A cat-shaped silhouette appeared on the ceiling above her, looking much like a shadow projected from an old slide projector. Debbie grabbed her cell phone and took a photo of it. The silhouette slowly faded over the next ten minutes as more and more light filtered through the window. Then, similar to the rainbow, the last hint of the cat shadow vanished, overwhelmed by the dawn.

Not long after, on a late night in August, Debbie went to bed, but, before she fell asleep, as was her habit, she reviewed tomorrow's to-do list and her upcoming writing projects in her head.

The bedroom light was off and she had her eyes closed when a sound, like the padding of cat feet, caught her attention. She opened her eyes and looked toward the door. Out of the corner of her eye, on the floor beside the bed, Debbie glimpsed a grayish cat shape—not a real cat, but the shadow of one. Not fully awake, at first she assumed it was one of her three kitties, but, as she looked directly at it, it vanished. She got up and looked for her flesh-and-blood cats, but none were nearby. She wondered, did she really see a cat on the ceiling? What about the cat on the floor? Was it her imagination, lack of sleep or a dream? The vision of the cat was so brief; she dismissed it as fatigue and slipped off to sleep.

Around the same time, Debbie's fifteen-year-old daughter was visited by a ghost cat in her own bedroom. Well past midnight, the teenager sat on her bedroom floor. Out of the corner of her eye, she caught a glimpse of a cat just chilling by the doorway, looking as if it wanted to be fed or petted. Similar to Debbie's sighting, the teenager saw the cat in her peripheral vision, and then, as she turned her head to look directly at it, it disappeared. Unlike Debbie's gray-shaded ghost cat, her daughter's apparition appeared white.

It couldn't have been one of their housecats. While years before, the room used to be a popular hangout for the family felines, Debbie's daughter had recently started crocheting. Filled with sewing needles and skeins of yarn and other tantalizing but deadly hazards, all four-footed family members were banned from the bedroom. With the door closed at all times, the teenager's personal space had turned into a cat-free zone. The girl had no idea who the little white cat was or where it went.

Days later, Debbie saw her ghost again. This time, the appearance took place on the cat tree in the bedroom next to hers. Debbie used the space as a combination office and cat room. The office held her desk and file cabinet, and for the cats' benefit, a litter box, cat toys, and a tattered three-level cat tree.

It was early dawn. Debbie was getting ready for work. Passing the open office door, Debbie felt a presence inside. Early morning sunlight creeping past the drapes gave the room an eerie, shadowy effect. As she angled into the room, Debbie again saw something out the corner of her eye—a cat sitting on the top level of the cat tree. In the semi-darkness, she thought it might be Stripey or Harry, but it had the same shape and smoky shade as the phantom on her bedroom floor. When she looked closer, it puffed into air. Whatever it was, it hadn't left the room in the normal manner.

A search of the office turned up no cat. She checked the living room and found all three cats nonchalantly waiting for their breakfast. She'd been standing in the doorway, so she knew it hadn't jumped off the tree or dashed past her feet into the hall. Since the image only lasted a second, once again she chalked it up to her imagination. "It was hard for me to believe," she said.

A week later, Debbie's daughter mentioned her encounter with the white ghost cat in her bedroom. What a relief! The truth had set Debbie free. Since they both had seen the ghost cat, Debbie knew she wasn't crazy.

Not too long after Debbie and her daughter shared their experiences, Debbie and her husband sat at the kitchen table. All three of their living cats were in other parts of the house. As they talked, Debbie glimpsed the shadow of a cat by the food bowls. At first, she wondered which of their cats was eating, but again when she turned her head, there was no cat.

At that same moment, her paranormally skeptical hubby reacted as if he had witnessed something extraordinary. He had. He described seeing a flash by the cat food area. "It must be a ghost cat," he admitted. "It wasn't one of our cats. Whatever it was, it didn't leave the kitchen."

"So you saw it, too?" Debbie asked.

Indeed he had!

At last, vindication! Her skeptical husband had seen the spirit cat at the same time she had. Debbie felt such relief. As they sat and stared at the food bowls, Debbie finally told him about her experiences in the bedroom and the office.

For the De Louise family, the ghost cat sightings came in small clusters. The cat ghost made several appearances over a couple of weeks, and then six months passed before they saw it again. There would follow another group of visits, followed by another dry spell.

Debbie believes the appearance of the cat on the ceiling was a message from either her mother or Oliver. They've lost other cats in the house, so neither she nor her daughter really knew who the gray or the white spirits were. However, they do enjoy seeing their little ghost cat and always look forward to the next visit.

*****

Debbie De Louise is a librarian at a public library on Long Island and the author of ten novels, including the Cobble Cove cozy mystery series featuring a librarian and a library cat. She is a member of the Cat Writers' Association and is owned by three cats. Learn more about her and her books at debbiedelouise.com.

"He rewrites everything I do! He must have been an editor in one of his previous nine lives!"

CHAPTER 4: MANY HAPPY RETURNS

Have you ever met someone for the first time, but in your heart you feel as if you've met them before? —Joanne Kenrick

    Many cat lovers have lost their best friends, only to have them return not in spirit, but in the flesh. Perhaps not the same flesh, but flesh nevertheless. In other words, reincarnation.
    Reincarnation is the rebirth of the life force within a new physical body. A reborn soul may have some personality traits and physical similarities in common with his former self, but it's not a stretch that with entirely different DNA and different life experiences, Fluffy

would still look and act uniquely. You may be able to bring home a kitty who's the same breed or color as Fluffy, but never a cat who looks and acts exactly like him.

Even a 100 percent genetic clone isn't an exact replica of the original DNA donor. The first cloned cat, CC (short for Carbon Copy or Copy Cat), was a brown tabby and white cat whose donor cell came from a calico named Rainbow. Despite sharing Rainbow's exact DNA, CC looked nothing like her. There are many environmental factors that affect coat patterns and different life experiences affect behavior.[6] Bonus question: Do Rainbow and CC have different souls? Inquiring minds want to know.

If a reincarnated cat isn't exactly the same, how will you know him? In some cases, a person simply looks in the cat's eyes and recognizes this is an old friend. Others need a sign.

Pay attention to his personality and habits, his likes and dislikes. Does the new kitty share a specific behavior that was unique to your late kitty—even for just a short while? Perhaps there is an idiosyncrasy your past kitty had—one you haven't seen before in other cats—and the new cat does this naturally without training or encouragement. Does he do a lot of the same things from his past life? Is he afraid of the same things? Perhaps he loves a certain unique treat, is attracted to Fluffy's favorite toy, or sleeps in his predecessor's favorite spot. Maybe he lounges with his paws crossed or hangs his head off the bed as Fluffy always did.

Sometimes, once you've had your family reunion, the trait disappears. Even so, you and Fluffy are together again. Don't be disappointed if the relationship isn't the exactly the same. Simply enjoy your new life together.

The Baby Sitter

Riou, a large tuxedo cat with slick fur, came to Weems Hutto as a

---

[6] https://drsophiayin.com/blog/entry/cloning-cats-rainbow-and-cc-prove-that-cloning-wont-resurrect-your-pet

tiny kitten. Weems had never had a pet before when he decided it was time for a kitty companion. In 1978, when rescue shelters were rare in Chicago, he went to a shopping mall pet store in downtown Evanston, Illinois, to find his new best friend. From his research, Weems read that females didn't spray urine, so he was on the hunt for a girl kitty.

On his first trip, the pet store didn't have any kittens, but on his second visit they had four eight-week-olds from the same litter. The employee pointed out a little tuxedo. "This one's a girl," she told the future cat daddy.

Weems took the tuxedo kitty he named Skritch, along with the usual kitty necessities. Not only was she friendly and curious, she was quite talkative. The kitten's favorite word wasn't "meow" but a trilled "ree-u." She quickly settled into his small apartment.

His cat care book recommended taking a new kitten to the vet as soon as possible, so Weems took Skritch to a nearby clinic for her vaccinations. That was when Weems learned his sweet little girl kitty had a couple of extra accessories under "her" tail. With the gender reassignment, Weems decided to change the name to Riou (pronounced *ree-you*, the same as the kitten's favorite word.) When Riou matured he had a large nose and markings that resembled a black beard.

Like all kittens, Riou loved to scratch the back of the couch, which eventually produced a hole in the upholstery. The opening gave him the perfect place to take a nap undisturbed. He loved his sofa hide-a-bed.

Weems worked long hours and decided his then two-year-old Riou needed a kitty companion, so he adopted a six-week-old calico kitten he named Eiu (because that was what she said.) Riou fell head over paws in love with the kitten. From the moment he met Eiu, Riou took care of her. He bathed her; he played ever so gently with her; they snuggled and slept together.

Years later Weems married; he, Riou, Eiu, and the other kitties he'd rescued along the way, moved into his new wife's home in north Texas. Shortly after the move, they lost Eiu to fatty liver disease. Over the years, the couple fostered numerous bottle babies, and Riou loved caring for the kittens until they were old enough to go to their forever homes. He took great pleasure in bathing and snuggling with the kittens, as he had with Eiu. In early 1997, Riou's health declined. He was laid to rest at the age of nineteen.

Months later, the family bought another house in a nearby town.

After the move, there was a large feline family turnover, as elderly cats crossed the Rainbow Bridge and foster failures became permanent residents.

One Sunday morning Weems's wife, Dusty, stopped by PetSmart to pick up cat litter. As was her habit, she stopped at the cat adoption cages to check out the new arrivals. She made a quick mental note of the cats available for adoption, in case potential adopters called her looking for a specific breed or color of cat. As she passed a stack of cages, someone tapped her on her right shoulder. She turned around, expecting to see a fellow rescuer.

She gasped. Reaching for her through the bars of the cage was Riou, or at least Riou's doppelgänger. A large tuxedo cat with a beard, he had a prominent proboscis and bright green eyes. His arm relaxed, but the paw remained extended as far as he could reach. He really wanted her attention.

Dusty asked the volunteer if she could hold the kitty. Within a few seconds the nine-month-old kitten melted into her arms. He felt like an old friend, someone who had been with her before. Unlike most adolescent kittens, who after a minute or so squirm to get down, this cat closed his eyes and lived deeply in the moment.

Dusty didn't believe in reincarnation—at all—but this cat knew her and she knew the cat, even though they had never met before. She couldn't explain it. She and Weems had six cats between them. They didn't need to add another feline family member. It didn't matter. As if she had no control over her actions, she found herself filling out the adoption application and giving the volunteer a check for the adoption fee. She and Weems had fostered kittens for the group, so no home visit was necessary.

She didn't even have a carrier in the car. She let him loose in her Outback. She called home and left a message on the voicemail. "Hi, I'll be home in a few minutes." In the background, loud meows punctuated each word.

When she arrived home, Weems was still off on a thirty-mile bicycle ride. That would give her time to come up with a plan. Rather than isolate the cat, as she knew she should do, she released him in the living room. Something strange happened. All the cats who had known Riou walked past him with nonchalance, as if to say, "Hey, where ya been?" The cats who had joined the household after Riou's passing approached him and hissed. The new cat investigated the house like an explorer, checking out every cabinet and hiding place. If this was Riou, of course he wouldn't recognize this house; the couple moved there after he passed.

After the cat's expedition, Dusty placed him in the master bathroom with food, water, a litter box, and . . . cat litter. The reason for her visit to PetSmart, but she forgot to pick it up.

A few minutes later Weems arrived home, tired and sweaty from his long ride in the hot Texas sun. He came out of the bathroom. "Where'd the cat come from?"

"Uh—" Dusty had to word this carefully. "Near PetSmart. Very near."

"Okay." Weems was never one to turn away a cat in trouble.

A little while later, Dusty confessed. "I got him *very* near PetSmart. Inside PetSmart."

"Take him back."

She explained the cat's introduction and how he behaved with the older cats. "If within twenty-four hours you don't think this is Riou, I'll return him," she promised. "There's another woman who wants to adopt him. He'll be fine."

They still needed cat litter, so Dusty ran to a nearby Petco. Before she checked out, she called Weems. "Do we need kitten food or not?"

She could hear him smile. "We have a kitten, don't we?"

Before she returned home, Weems had dubbed the big tuxedo Riou II.

It didn't take long for new Riou to find the sofa upstairs with the hole in the back big enough for him to enter. The first time, he disappeared for hours, and Weems feared Riou may have somehow escaped the house. After scouring the neighborhood, they finally found him sleeping soundly inside "his" old gray couch. This Riou lucked out, because Weems had a cat fence installed that allowed the kitties to go into the backyard without risking escape. Using the cat flap, the kitties could enjoy the outdoors at will.

The Huttos continued to foster neonatal kittens. Not long after his adoption, Weems and Dusty took in a litter of three-hours-old kittens. Riou II got super excited about the newborns, and became the self-appointed baby sitter. When his new humans weren't watching, Riou II snuck into the neonatal bathroom (nursery), swiped a kitten and carried it upstairs where he gave it a thorough bath. The neonate screamed and raised a ruckus.

Another litter of orphans, arriving when they were only hours old, were especially adorable to the tuxedo. Two of the tinies were normal, but one simply wasn't right. Later they learned that not only was he deaf, he also suffered from hydrocephaly, water on the brain.

This kitten never vocalized.

As usual, Riou swiped one of the kittens for bath time. When Dusty noticed the tabby kitten was missing, she followed the sound of the crying kitten into the backyard, where Uncle Riou snuggled and bathed him. She put the kitten back with his two brothers. A little while later, she checked on them and this time the tuxedo kitten, who didn't vocalize, was missing. After another intensive cat hunt, she found the tiny tuxedo in the backyard being nurtured by Uncle Riou.

As the kittens came and went, Uncle Riou raised them, teaching them manners and socialization. Riou lived combined lives of three and a half decades. After many happy years and many hundreds of foster kittens to care for, Riou made his second trip across the Rainbow Bridge. He must have finished his business. He hasn't been back.

Mom, Is That You?

Edy Chandler wanted a Siamese kitten so badly. And what doting father could resist a five-year-old's request? So Edy's dad, Henry, took his daughter to a Siamese breeder to find a feline companion. The woman had the perfect kitten—an affectionate six-week-old cutie who didn't have what it took to be a show cat. Edy instantly fell in love with the sweet little seal point with a kinked tail and slightly crossed blue eyes. Edy named her Kipper.

However, when they arrived home with Kipper, Edy's mom was less than thrilled. Ceil (short for Cecelia) was no fan of cats; in less than a year Edy had to rehome her little buddy. Letting Kipper go was one of the hardest things Edy ever do in her entire life. As she said goodbye to her cat, she vowed she would never love anything like that again. For decades, she kept her vow. And despite having to give up her kitty, Edy maintained a close relationship with her mom for the rest of Ceil's life.

Ceil, of Polish and Russian descent, had dark brown eyes, almost black, and dark brown hair worn short. As Mom grew older, her hair darkened to almost a jet black. On several occasions, Ceil confessed to her daughter that she had always wanted green eyes and auburn hair. Before Edy was born, Ceil put henna in her hair to give it a reddish sheen.

Ceil was the sort of person who was never intimidated, and she said precisely what was on her mind. When she spoke, her voice carried. Edy described her as forceful, always direct; she did not speak softly.

As Edy's mom aged, she developed thyroid issues. A year before her passing, Ceil told her daughter, "You're going to miss me when I'm gone." When Ceil first said that, Edy certainly didn't know how ill her mother really was. Edy believes Ceil didn't know either, but her arteries were severely clogged. She suffered a series of mini strokes.

Doctors performed surgery to clear the blockages, but during the procedure Ceil suffered a massive stroke. For a month Ceil was comatose and then in a semi-coma for another month. She improved, but the stroke left Ceil paralyzed on her left side and robbed her of the ability to speak. No matter how hard she tried, attempts to talk only resulted in gibberish. Ceil was so frustrated that she stopped trying to communicate at all.

After Ceil's stroke, Edy decided that living under one roof would make it easier for her to take care of her parents, so she rented an apartment with enough room for both her mom and dad, who was also struggling with health issues. Because Mom couldn't eat on her own, Edy hand-fed her at every meal. One evening, Edy made spaghetti and blended it into a paste. At one point Ceil was so done with everything, she mustered all her faculties and simply said, "Edith, enough."

Eight months after the ill-fated surgery, Ceil's liver began to fail. She died at four in the morning at the age of 72. When Edy woke up that morning she already knew her mother was gone. Henry woke complaining of chest pain, although he didn't know the cause.

Following her mom's death, Edy went to work in a Houston-area cat hospital as the clinic office manager. Naturally, working in a cat hospital, she was surrounded by many wonderful felines in need of homes. Edy didn't want a cat. It had been many decades, but she still remembered the pain of letting Kipper go. That was not going to happen again.

One afternoon in late 1999, she went into the surgical holding area. In one of the top cages sat the clinic's newest permanent resident, Levitan's Sweet Necessity of Rextinue.

A few days earlier Doc had brought the Oriental Shorthair to the clinic to expand her breeding program. Nessy, as everyone lovingly referred to her, had a stunning chestnut smoke (almost black) coat with bright green eyes and enormous ears. She looked like a little fruit bat.

The instant Edy walked near the cages, Nessy began to scream at her. Edy opened the cage and out popped Nessy into Edy's arms. In that moment, the two formed an unbreakable connection.

It wasn't long before Doc called Nessy "Edy's cat." Edy wasn't interested. Nessy was quite a valuable cat and, once again, she didn't want to get too attached. But the heart wants what the heart wants, and Nessy knew exactly what she wanted.

Edy fought the inevitable for three years. Any time she walked by Nessy's enclosure, the kitty would scream until Edy took her out and held her. After two failed attempts to breed Nessy, she developed the uterine infection pyometra. She was spayed and Doc needed to find a home for her.

One afternoon, Edy was looking at Nessy. She had those amazing green eyes, and at certain angles under the fluorescent lighting, Nessy's coat had a purple sheen. Edy remembered her mom telling her on so many occasions that she always wished she had green eyes and auburn hair. Seeing the green-eyed cat was kind of ironic, but she dismissed the idea as mere coincidence.

Finally, Doc insisted Edy take Nessy home to be a companion for Edy and her dad. Nessy instantly befriended Henry and became his companion. She wanted to be close to him and often lay over his heart.

After Henry passed, Edy and Nessy resumed their close friendship. When Edy returned home from work, she and Nessy often shared in-depth conversations. Edy said something and Nessy responded with a vocalization that sounded like a moo. Sometimes the cat honked. Nessy always got her point across. She was also very astute; nothing got past her and she noticed everything. Like Ceil, Nessy was bossy and demanded Edy's full attention. She was opinionated and communicated everything at almost full volume.

At home, Edy often shared time with Nessy by the fluorescent light in the kitchen, where her coat took on that purplish glow. Edy kept thinking about the green eyes, the color of her hair, and wondered, was it possible? The more time she spent around the little cat, the clearer it became that Nessy was channeling Ceil.

As the months passed, Edy began to believe in the possibility of the Ceil/Nessy connection, but in Nessy's final six months, she knew for certain her mother had come back to keep her company.

Shortly after Henry passed, Nessy was diagnosed with breast cancer. Doc removed the lump, but Nessy developed a post-surgery infection. To treat the infection, Nessy had to lie on her back, tummy up, front paws draped over the vet tech's arm, to allow the tech to saturate the wound with penicillin. Edy stood nearby to comfort Nessy during the fifteen-minute treatment. For eight minutes, Nessy silently accepted the manhandling. Then she looked up at the tech, and vocalized "Mmmmmmmm?" with a question mark at the end, as if asking, "How much longer?" Edy and the vet tech stared at each other. In all her years as a tech, she had never had anything like that happen. Once again, Nessy had shown her human side.

About six months before Nessy passed, she began acting even more like Ceil. The moment Edy walked in the door after work, Nessy screamed at her demanding attention. Phone conversations with friends were interrupted. Nessy vocalized and circled Edy's feet as she stood there talking on the phone. Edy picked her up, and told her, echoing her mother's words, "Yes, I know, pay attention to you. You're not going to be here much longer, and I will miss you when you are gone." Nessy responded with a thunderous purr.

At the time, Edy didn't know her kitty's cancer had returned and her heart was failing. Edy knew beyond any doubt that Nessy was her mother in kitty clothes, with the green eyes and auburn highlights she had always wanted.

Nessy lost her battle with cancer in 2010. And yes, Edy missed her doubly, because she knew she'd said goodbye to both Ceil and Nessy. Nessy's ashes are kept in a black porcelain cat-shaped urn next to Edy's home computer and Nessy's face greets Edy every morning on the computer screens at both work and at home. She believes that through Nessy, her mother was with her for a just a little longer.

*****

Edy Chandler is the office manager at All Cats Veterinary Clinic in Houston. An artist, she produces fine art in a variety of mediums including hand-made beaded necklaces, as well as colored pencil, acrylic, and tempera. Of course, she loves her kitties.

The Ceiling Fan Gremlin

Tracy Big Pond loves two things: cats and fun movies.

Although she gravitated more toward science fiction, fantasy, and action flicks, Tracy was a big fan of the Steven Spielberg horror/comedy *Gremlins*, about a teenage boy who is given a unique creature called a mogwai for Christmas. The kid names his new pet Gizmo. In the *Gremlins* universe, mogwai spawn if they get wet. Benign mogwai can transform into evil gremlins if they sneak a snack after midnight. In the movie, a water spill and accidental after-hours feeding transforms the sleepy town of Kingston Falls, New York, into a center of chaos and destruction at the claws of gremlins gone amok.

Tracy especially loved the scene at Dorry's Tavern. As music blared from the jukebox in the smoky bar, a gremlin wearing a red stocking cap hung from the blade of a ceiling fan, revolving around and around and around. Who didn't love a cute little flying monster wearing a Santa hat?

Over the years, Tracy watched the movie at least five times. She liked the idea that the mogwai are really supposed to be a force for good. She even gave her son, Jimmy, the childhood nickname Mogwai.

A decade after the movie was released, one of Tracy's coworkers had an unspayed cat who had been entertaining a traveling salescat and now they had an unexpected litter of kittens. The coworker knew Tracy was a soft touch, so she offered her one of the kittens.

Tracy really wasn't looking for a kitty. After all, they already had three cats. She really didn't need more responsibility, and besides, she knew her hubby would kill her. Maybe not in the literal, life-ending sense, but there would certainly be a loud exchange of ideas. Her gut told her she should take a look at the kittens, so she did. After all, her son Jimmy, now in sixth grade, would be so excited about a new kitten!

The litter was six weeks old, mostly tuxedos and tabbies. Tracy sat on the floor, where the kittens behaved like awkward teenagers trying too hard to impress a potential date. The squirming, furry mass tripped over one another, vying for her attention. But Tracy quickly homed in on the more reserved runt of the litter with the exotic body markings. The mostly white kitten had black patches on the back of his legs that looked as if he'd sat in a puddle of wet paint. He also wore a black baseball cap that rested on his fuzzy white head cockeyed and backwards. Tracy would later learn this unique set of markings is called a Van pattern, after the Turkish Van breed the pattern is named after.

Playing hard-to-get seemed to be that kitten's strategy. With the finesse of an experienced fisherman, he toyed with Tracy from a distance. He gave her a soft nip to the finger, and she was instantly hooked. He reeled her in, and she adopted the kitten with the attitude on the spot.

Before she could say, "Don't feed him after midnight," she was climbing into her car with the kitten in her arms. What was she doing? Her entire life she had been drawn to black cats. And as an adult, she'd never owned anything but solid black felines. How would her other cats (one male and two females) react?

For the fifteen-minute ride home, Tracy put the kitten in a cat carrier, but he immediately began yowling. At her first opportunity, she pulled over and freed him. Once liberated, he enjoyed riding in the car. He briefly explored the vehicle, then sprang onto Tracy's shoulder. For the rest of the trip home, he rode nestled beneath her long auburn hair. As they drove, the kitten stared out the windows and growled at other vehicles speeding past his car.

At home, it didn't take long for the kitten to settle into his new environment. Despite his petite stature, he quickly wrapped his feline housemates around his little claws.

But what should they name him? Tracy didn't know yet. And she wasn't in a hurry; when he was ready, the new kitty would reveal his name to her. They always did. It just took time, patience, and a good power of observation.

Two weeks later, Tracy's husband, Robert, brought the kitten upstairs and placed him on Tracy's chest. Just ten minutes earlier, she tried to snuggle with him and he wasn't having any of it. "He won't stay," she told Robert.

"He will now," he laughed.

Against her skin she felt the kitten's heartbeat, a very rapid thump-thump, thump-thump.

"What did you do to him?" Tracy demanded, fearing her sometimes mischievous husband may have teased the kitten.

"I didn't do anything!"

A few minutes earlier, Robert had started up the stairs on the way to their bedroom when he saw something out of the corner of his eye. He turned to look but didn't see anything, so he went up a couple of steps. Once again, he thought he saw something for an instant. At the top of the stairs, he turned on the light.

Hanging by one paw, the white and black kitten clung to one of the ceiling fan blades. It was anyone's guess how he got there. Maybe he launched himself off the bannister and latched on as he flew past the fan. After Robert stopped laughing, he peeled the kitten from the blade and brought him to Tracy.

Her husband's vivid and funny description took her back to the movie's ceiling fan gremlin in the smoke-filled pub. Tracy burst into laughter. The kitten had finally revealed his name: Gizmo, the benign alter-ego of the malevolent gremlins who took over Kingston Falls in the movie.

A devout foodie, the once-delicate runt eventually grew into a twenty-two pound bruiser who tended to throw his weight around with the other cats. Fortunately, he started channeling the gentler mogwai after Tracy had him separated from his testicles.

Over the next year, Tracy discovered that although their new family member wasn't a fan of being held, he followed her around the house like a puppy. Gizmo never went outside, but one day when gazing through the window, Tracy began to think, "If he acts like a puppy, maybe I could take him for a walk." After acclimating him to a harness, Tracy trained Gizmo to walk on a leash. A short time later, Jimmy got an iguana, who Tracy also trained to walk on a harness and leash. Together, the odd foursome often went on strolls together.

Gizmo enjoyed riding in the car whenever Tracy drove her son, Jimmy, and his friends around. The other kids even referred to Gizmo as their "little brother." He also played fetch with his cat toys. He often dragged Jimmy's stuffed animals down the hall, laying them out in a line in descending order of size.

Gizmo's acute sense of hearing could pick up the sound of a cellophane candy wrapper almost anywhere in the house. He immediately appeared for the chance to bat it around. He had a fascination for water. He even occasionally climbed into the tub when the humans were trying to take a shower. Tracy eventually learned that these characteristics were typical breed traits of

Turkish Vans.

Gizmo was only a year old when a freak accident at home took his life. After he passed, Tracy visited a website about cat breeds, just out of curiosity. She entered all of Gizmo's crazy characteristics, and the site said she should get a Turkish Van.

Twenty-two years after Gizmo's death, Tracy found a breeder in Michigan who had a litter of Turkish Van kittens. The woman sent pictures, and Tracy fell in love with the boy with the white coat and a blue-gray Van-pattern with a beautiful blue tail. Who couldn't love the swooping pattern on the left side of his head and those icy azure eyes? Just as she had been with Gizmo, Tracy was hooked.

When the kitten was old enough to take home, Tracy drove fourteen hours to Michigan to pick him up. But she struggled with her decision. Even after twenty-two years, she really wasn't ready to replace Gizmo. Throughout the endlessly long ride home to Oklahoma, she alternated between tears over losing Gizmo and joy over the new kitten.

Like his predecessor, the sixteen-week-old kitten was no fan of the carrier, so Tracy let him out in the car. As Gizmo had done, he quickly checked out the car, then sat next to her.

She offered the kitten food and water, which he shunned in favor of her taco. Nothing resembling food was safe around him. On that long drive, the kitten discovered the allure of drinking straws. Tracy had to shield her soft drink cup with a sack to keep him from stealing the straws.

After the next fast food stop, she had to guard her hamburger from the assertive kitten. "I know you," Tracy told her new kitten. As Tracy pried the kitten away from her food, she said, "You're a Daemon!" As she moved him, he still managed to snap and grab a mouthful of tasty all-beef patty.

With the kitten still chewing his stolen food, Tracy asked him his name. She felt the response: "You already know it. I waited to come back. You don't know it yet, but you're going to really need me soon."

While Tracy napped in the front seat of her car, she began to call him by his proper name, Gizmo. At other times, he was Daemon. Instinctively, the kitten responded to Gizmo. When she called him Daemon, in a typical cat response, he ignored her. Her mental wheels began to turn. This kitten was more like a gremlin than a demon. Gremlin it is.

At home, Gremlin showed Tracy even more of his Gizmo side. When it came time to teach him to walk on a leash, Gremlin already knew the drill, walking like a pro from the moment she put the harness on him. Like his predecessor, he often dragged the dog's stuffed animals to his pet cemetery and killed them. (Apparently, he doesn't feel the need to sort them by size.)

Gremlin also has Gizmo's Turkish Van obsession with water. He almost always hops in the shower with Tracy. If she wants to have the shower to herself, she has to lock her Gremlin out of the bathroom. If the tub isn't occupied, he carries his toys in his mouth, dashing back and forth through the open door between his room and the bathroom, finally dropping them in the tub and kicking them around.

As Gremlin had warned Tracy that first day, she did need him. He helped her through the stressful period when Tracy cared for her grandma, who struggled with dementia. Grandma's decline was hard on Tracy and her passing was devastating.

Today, Gremlin uses his powers for good. The healing energy of his purr eases Tracy's physical and emotional pain. He even coordinates purr power healing sessions with the other cats. Tara, the lightest cat, rests on Tracy's chest, while Gremlin, with his powerful purr, positions himself next to the area that hurts the most.

Tracy knows Gizmo is back for the second of his nine lives. She hopes it's a long time before he has to return for the third time.

*****

Tracy Big Pond is from Stillwater, Oklahoma. She has an incredible son and a beautiful granddaughter. She lives with a couple of pedigreed Turkish Van cats, a couple of rescue kitties, and a couple of Australian Shepherds, all of whom graciously allow her to serve them in return for cuddles, head-butts and viewing hilarious antics.

"We have a pet now. The house came with a ghost cat."

CHAPTER 5: NOT MY GHOST CAT

Prowling his own quiet backyard or asleep by the fire, he is still only a whisker away from the wilds. —Jean Burden, *Celebration of Cats*

Who doesn't love the photos on social media taken by people who just came home to find a cat lounging confidently on their sofa or snoozing on their bed? The only problem—the person taking the photo doesn't have a cat!

Something similar sometimes occurs when families move into a new place. Whether it's a house, apartment, or dorm, you never know what the previous residents are going to leave behind for you to pick up. Some people accidently forget treasured family mementos; others leave behind a paranormal entity or two. Sometimes they have four paws and whiskers.

Numerous ghost cat stories were sent to me from people who were surprised that their new home came with the perfect pet—a ghost cat. You don't have to nag the kids to feed him, he doesn't shed fur or dander, and he doesn't need the litter box scooped.

Mystery Cat/Guardian Angel

Jean Marie Ward's first encounter with the spectral cat who inhabits her home happened as they were moving into their new house, a mid-twentieth-century single-family home in Alexandria, Virginia. As she carried a stack of boxes through the kitchen door, watching her feet to make sure she didn't trip, a light-colored animal streaked past her legs and into the kitchen. It moved so quickly that she only caught a glimpse. It could have been any frightened wild animal; it might have been a cat.

A huge variety of wildlife lived on the property, and she didn't want some wild bunny gnawing on computer cables, a raccoon pooping on the carpet, or a squirrel eating through the electrical wiring in the attic. When she inspected the corner of the kitchen where the white blur paused, there was nothing there. Just in case, she told Greg, her husband, there might be a cat loose in the house. A thorough search of the entire home came up empty, so she dismissed the streak as a trick of the light, then promptly forgot about it.

At least for a couple weeks, until it happened again. This time, however, she caught a glimpse of the culprit—a little shorthaired, gray and white critter, which vanished the instant she looked at it straight on. It *was* a cat! She couldn't see through it, but it wasn't as substantial as a living creature. When it blinked out of view, she realized they might be living with a spectral pet. She thought, "Oh, that's why we couldn't find it."

It took her a while to finally tell Greg they had a ghost cat. She wanted to be sure her imagination wasn't running amok or the light playing tricks. After all, no one else visiting the home admitted to seeing it, even friends who considered themselves psychic. Not that Greg wouldn't have believed her. He'd had his own experiences from beyond the grave. As a boy, he received a personal goodbye from his grandfather who had just passed.

When she finally accepted that they were living with a ghost kitty, she decided that of all the things that could haunt their home, a ghost cat was the nicest possibility.

From her brief encounters, Jean Marie got the impression that the ghost cat was female, but it's sometimes hard to tell feline gender, even with living cats. Had she been a real cat, she wouldn't have weighed more than seven or eight pounds.

Curious, Jean Marie spoke to the wife of the man who built the house and asked if any of the former owners had a cat. The wife thought one of the previous residents had one, but couldn't remember any details.

The apparition became a regular visitor after that. It acted like a shy but playful living cat. The behavior was always the same: Ghost Cat would dash into a room, Jean Marie caught a cat shape out of the corner of her eye, but before she could focus on it, the cat disappeared. Some visits were longer than others; they mostly lasted just a few seconds.

Over the next ten years, the little ghost appeared intermittently. Early on, she showed up every few weeks, then gradually visits became less frequent—every couple of months. Ghost Cat usually appeared when Jean Marie was tired or stressed, or just needed a smile. The cat's appearance never failed to lift her mood.

It seldom showed itself to anyone but Jean Marie. However, after several years passed, a cat-loving friend named Kate visited Jean Marie for the first time since the move. The women hunkered down with tea and pastries at the dining room table, talking for hours about their families, jobs, books, TV... everything except ghosts. But when Jean Marie returned from the kitchen after brewing their second pot of tea, Kate nearly jumped out of her chair. Her eyes were wild.

Jean Marie set the teapot on the table. Keeping her voice casual, she simply asked, "Gray and white?"

Kate let out a deep breath. "Yeah."

"Little thing—five to eight pounds?" Jean Marie's friend eyed her suspiciously. Jean Marie said, "Ghost cat."

"Oh, thank God!" Kate said. "I was beginning to wonder if I was seeing things. I didn't think you'd get a cat without telling me, but it kept darting in and out of my field of vision."

"I think it was checking you out," Jean Marie said.

"Did I pass?"

"Well, you're the first person other than me to talk about it."

For well over half an hour, Kate's head swiveled to different corners of the room trying to catch a good look at the ghost watching from a distance.

GHOST CATS 2

After Kate's visit, ghost kitty sightings grew less frequent. By the time Jean Marie and her husband adopted their first corporeal cat, Jean Marie couldn't remember the last time she'd seen the little gray and white.

The live cat was a ten-year-old kitty whose owner had recently died. Several months after Duzell (also known as Our Most Benevolent Feline Overlord) joined the family, Jean Marie had her final encounter with their spectral pet. Duzell liked to sleep in a bed warmed by the body heat of his human servants. It took only a short time before His Benevolence trained Jean Marie and Greg to leave the bedroom door open so he could move about the house freely in the wee hours. Jean Marie had grown accustomed to the distinctive thump of the twelve-pound black-and-white cat landing on the corner of the bed and stalking across the comforter. So she didn't think anything of it when one night she felt a thump and the poke, poke, poke, poke of little cat feet negotiating the covers. But something was off. She looked up and noticed His Benevolence sitting in the doorway. At the foot of the bed was . . . nothing—unless you counted the cat paw-sized depressions in the comforter. While there was no visible cat, Jean Marie felt the weight of a cat and the catlike warmth. She gulped. It's one thing to know your house is haunted by a spectral cat. But . . . on . . . the . . . bed . . . while you're in it!

Once she got over her initial shock, though, there was no sense of menace. It was just . . . weird.

Disgusted by his human's cowardice, Duzell flicked his tail against the floor. He leaped onto the bed and padded to his customary spot at Jean Marie's side. The Ghost Cat squished herself into a little ball by Jean Marie's feet.

Jean Marie knew the experience wasn't a night terror. She was fully awake and mobile the whole time. She even deliberately petted His Benevolence to prove she could.

There, the three of them lay together until Greg joined them a couple of hours later. He tried to tell Jean Marie she was dreaming, but she insisted he turn on the light. There, by the light of the overhead lamp, the footprints remained, as did a cat-sized crater in the comforter next to Jean Marie's feet. It was a puffy comforter and they both saw the depression in the fabric. The sensation of a warm, weighted body was gone, however.

Jean Marie never saw the gray and white cat again. She worried she may have hurt the ghost's feelings.

"I felt sad," she said. "At first I didn't think I chased it away, but I may have."

While that was the last time Jean Marie experienced the little ghost cat, it wasn't the end of the story. The other living beings in the house still engaged with Ghost Cat from time to time. Greg, who was prone to migraines, often napped downstairs. Sometimes he found he was sharing the bed in the basement bedroom with the ghost cat. On other occasions, Jean Marie caught Duzell attentively eyeing an empty space in the middle of the carpet or gently pressing his nose against a cat-sized something that wasn't there. Jean Marie knew he was interacting with Ghost Cat.

After five happy years with Jean Marie and Gregg, Duzell came to the end of his life. The veterinarian came to the house and put him to sleep in the place where he felt happy and safe. After they lost Duzell, Greg said Ghost Cat never again joined him for a nap. They are convinced the ghost and Duzell finally had a chance to play face-to-face and groom each other.

*****

Jean Marie Ward (JeanMarieWard.com) writes fiction, nonfiction, and everything in between. Her credits include a multi-award-nominated novel, numerous short stories, two popular art books, and a continuing interview series for Galaxy's Edge (GalaxysEdge.com).

Ghost Cat and the Evil Shadow

Ethan Nahté moved into a house with a past, but that didn't really bother him. He was just glad to find a place close to work with reasonable rent.

The old farmhouse sat in a large Arkansas field, between Mena and miniscule unincorporated Dallas, Arkansas. The property is close to what is now Highway 8 and runs along Long's Trail, which was in centuries past was a main thoroughfare for Wells Fargo, carrying people, mail, and cargo. In the 19th century, a creek that ran near the house had been a popular watering hole for stagecoach drivers and passengers.

The farmhouse was built in the mid-1940s. It began as a small two-bedroom with a kitchen and living room that housed a family of five. Through the years, the property provided a home for a menagerie of animals: horses, cattle, chickens, as well as hunting dogs and cats.

Eventually, the tiny home simply couldn't handle all the children and grandkids, so as the family expanded, so, too, did the house. They added living areas, bedrooms, and even a shower and an indoor toilet, ultimately doubling the size of the original structure. By the 1980s, the kids had grown up and left home, and only the elderly homeowners remained.

Like any aging wooden structure, the house made a great deal of noise. The hardwood floors creaked or squeaked whenever anyone walked from room to room.

When the elderly couple's health began to fail, a live-in healthcare assistant moved in, bringing with her a cat and a small dog. By then, the master bedroom went unused because the couple couldn't get in and out of their regular bed. The tall old man began sleeping in his outdated brown leather recliner in the living room, his long legs and large feet dangling over the footrest. The wife used an adjustable hospital bed in another bedroom.

One day, while the healthcare assistant was out running errands, the wife found her husband laid back in his recliner. She attempted to wake him, but he had passed away in his sleep.

Over the next few years, the cat died and the family moved the elderly grandmother into a nursing home. The grown brothers put up the house for rent, but left most of the furniture behind, including the recliner the old man died in.

Ethan Nahté worked for the youngest brother as a campground facilitator, and needed a place to rent—a real challenge in a small rural town where most people either kept the family house in perpetuity or sold it outright, but rarely rented.

Ethan moved into the farmhouse with Captain Crook, a four-month-old black-and-white kitten who had been dumped at the campground when she was just five weeks old. She had a black eye patch marking over one eye and a small crook at the end of her tail where it had been broken, so a pirate name seemed appropriate.

For some reason, when they first arrived, Crook was reluctant to go into the kitchen. Ethan set up her food and litter box at the far end of the utility room. After an hour or so, Crook calmed down, so Ethan assumed everything was fine.

One afternoon, Ethan took a break from unpacking boxes to do a little writing. He had set up his office in the bedroom that had been occupied by the healthcare worker. Because he was in the midst of unpacking and Ethan didn't want Crook's help, he sequestered her to the original part of the house, which gave her plenty of room to play and explore.

Ethan loves to write horror novels. When he wasn't at work, he would retreat to his office and enter the Writing Zone, that mental place where creativity flowed from his brain to his fingertips. Weeks of packing, moving, and then unpacking had kept him from writing, so he was eager to get back to work. As he tapped away at his keyboard, he caught a glimpse of movement out of the corner of his eye. He dismissed it as the shadow of a bird outside flying past the window.

A few minutes later, something brushed up against his leg beneath the desk. Glancing down, he caught sight of something black with a tail about shin-high. When he focused on the spot under the desk, he saw nothing. He scanned the room, expecting to find Crook, but found only stacks of boxes and a few unpacked items. Shrugging it off, he returned to his writing.

An hour or so later, he stood up to take a break when another black shadow shot across the room, darting from behind one box to another. Ethan rushed over to investigate. He was certain it was a cat.

He looked all about, calling to Crook, but still found nothing. He searched the living room for his kitten, thinking perhaps she had snuck into the office and was playing hide-and-seek. He found her lying atop the couch, lounging in the rays of the sun dancing between the slats of the blinds.

From then on, whenever Ethan went to work in his office, the ghost cat made an appearance. After several more sightings over the next few weeks, he caught more and more details of the mystery black cat. He saw it so many times that he sometimes called it Shadow, after a black cat he'd had as a child. It stuck to his office and rarely appeared in any other part of the house.

Like any cat, all interaction was on Shadow's terms. Ethan had to learn the rules. The little ghost would disappear if he stared directly at it for more than a few seconds. He also had to fight his instinct to touch it. If he tried to pet it when it rubbed against his legs, it vanished. When he stopped trying to interact with it, Shadow just hung out. It never let Ethan see it fully and it was always on the move. He tried taking a photo or video with his phone, but that also made the cat disappear.

Ethan wasn't Shadow's only friend. Every other week, Ethan trekked to Van Buren to visit his then-girlfriend, Lisa. Rather than disrupt Crook's life, Ethan's mom dropped by to feed and play with her. Several times, as Mom filled the food bowl, she felt a cat rub against her leg. When it first happened, Mom assumed it was Crook, but at the same instant, Crook strolled into the kitchen.

Lisa, on her biweekly visits to Ethan's place, also saw the ghost cat in his office. Sometimes, when she put on her makeup and had the bathroom door open, she caught a glimpse of the phantom kitty's reflection in the bathroom mirror.

Lisa also saw other entities in the house, but none as endearing as Shadow. Although Ethan never saw him, on several nights Lisa watched a spectral man walk down the dark hall from what was once the master bedroom. At first, Ethan suspected the figure might have been the elderly homeowner, but Lisa described him as a short man who seemed to project evil intentions. That description didn't fit the grandfather. Ethan wondered if this man may have had a connection to the stagecoaches that stopped nearby to water their horses.

One cold, wintery night, Ethan was sitting in the old man's recliner in the living room watching a movie. He wasn't bothered that the old man had died there; the chair was comfy. The TV screen and his cell phone screen provided the room's only light.

Captain Crook, by then a young adult, rested with her human, stretching from Ethan's knees to his chest. As Ethan texted Lisa, he caught a glimpse of the ghost cat dash across the living room, race away from the kitchen doorway toward his office, then disappeared through the closed wooden door. It caught him by surprise. It was the first and only time he'd seen Shadow in a room other than his office.

Instantly, the living room just felt "wrong." The room temperature dropped twenty degrees and goosebumps sprung up on Ethan's arms. At that same moment, Crook dug her claws into Ethan's shoulder before twisting herself around and landing on all fours in his lap. Back arched and hair erect, she stared at the entryway to the kitchen, hissing and digging her claws deeper into his legs. Whatever had terrified the ghost cat was now frightening Crook.

Ethan, too, sensed a presence. He looked toward the dark kitchen; an outdoor light gave a faint glow through the kitchen window—just enough to see the outline of a misshapen figure partially hidden by the doorway. For a moment, Ethan wondered if perhaps it was the original owner, but this bipedal form was no man. It reminded Ethan of photos he'd seen of alleged bigfoots.

He did a double take. He wanted to make sure he wasn't catching some odd reflection from the TV or the outside lights. The figure crouched slightly; were it fully erect, it would have stood taller than the doorway. Considering the entity's sheer bulk, Ethan was stunned that the obviously hairy black shape could conceal itself so well. Whatever it was, it surely couldn't be good.

The thing made no sound as it stared at Ethan and Crook with faintly glowing eyes. It felt as if it was boring a hole through him. Ethan switched his cell phone over to camera, hoping to capture proof of the entity that stood before him. He glanced at the camera icon and pressed it, then looked back up. In that brief instant, the figure had disappeared.

The room was silent, except for the movie playing in the background and the sound of Captain Crook hissing. Ethan knew any physical creature of that size would have made noise if it ran away. But silence reigned. A few seconds later, the temperature returned to normal. Crook relaxed her hold on Ethan's thigh. He stood up, dropping the cat from his lap, and she retreated behind the couch. The phone screen showed a fuzzy image of the room—nothing spectral in it. From Crook's reaction and the vibe it gave off, Ethan knew it was dark and malignant. He went from room to room making sure the doors and windows were locked. They were. This wasn't his first experience with a sinister spirit, so he was neither scared to be alone nor did he bother to turn the lights on.

Confident the house was secure, he returned his attention to the movie. Of course, he texted Lisa about the weird encounter. She responded that it might have been the old man that she saw in the hallway, but the descriptions didn't match.

Ethan lived in the old farmhouse for another eleven months, and never saw the evil figure again. He also never again saw his little shadow cat in that home.

Almost a year after seeing the figure in the kitchen, and two months before the COVID-19 pandemic hit, Ethan got a new job and moved in with Lisa a hundred miles away. She had never mentioned seeing anything out of the ordinary at her home—at least until Ethan moved in. One night, Ethan was sitting on the couch watching a movie, surrounded by Crook and Lisa's own cat and dog, when he spied something out of the corner of his eye.

"Did you see that?" he asked her.

She looked at him and replied, "A black cat?"

He nodded. "I think my ghost cat jumped in a box and moved with me."

She said, "I hope that's all you brought with you."

Fortunately, neither the old man nor the creepy dark figure ever appeared at Lisa's house.

For the entire eleven months Ethan stayed at Lisa's, both of them regularly glimpsed the ghost kitty. Ethan believes the ghost cat had no desire to remain in the old house with the dark entity. And, just as before, whenever Ethan started writing, the ghost cat dashed about and rubbed against Ethan's leg.

Ethan has since moved again, and now lives less than a mile from the old farmhouse, which recently sold. He's noticed the new owners have kicked the family's old possessions to the curb and often wonders if they have seen a presence, human or feline.

Crook is staying with Lisa, at least for now, as did the ghost cat. Lisa said on occasion she catches her own cat and Crook staring at the doorway between the living room and kitchen. When Lisa investigates, she often catches sight of the ghost cat. She said it is a sweet presence. She thinks it enjoys the company of the other cats. Ethan agrees. He believes the ghost cat simply wanted a friend or a family.

*****

Ethan Nahté is a speculative fiction writer, who also currently works as a production manager and editor for Pulse Multi-Media. He has also worked for several animal organizations, including directing a TV program for a no-kill shelter and as the executive director for a conservation organization. Check out his official author page at NahteWords.Wordpress.com. Better still, buy his books at www.NahteWords.com or check out his media company at www.livenloud.net.

Spooky Little Kitty

Lynne and George love the paranormal investigation shows on TV. They are such enthusiastic fans they even bought equipment so they could investigate the presence of a ghost, should the opportunity ever present itself. Until 2016, it hadn't. Then one night, as they watched an episode of *Ghost Adventures* on the desktop monitor in their upstairs office, Lynne and George distinctly heard a cat hiss from the floor directly behind them a foot or two away. At the same time, they both whipped around. Lynne asked her husband. "Did you hear a cat hiss?"

Not only did George hear it, but just a moment earlier he also heard the distinct sound of cat claws scratching a hard wooden object like the desk or the home's hardwood floors.

Their primary suspect was their only cat at the time, six-year-old Schrödinger, even though the large, mostly white cat never watched videos with them in the office.

They scanned the room, expecting to see their own cat, but Schrödinger was nowhere to be seen. After a quick search, they tracked him down in his favorite lounging spot, a basket in the hall outside the office. Roused from a sound sleep, Schrödinger blinked sleepily at them as if to say, "What's your problem?" One fact was certain; what they had heard wasn't Schrödinger.

The sound definitely hadn't come from outside the townhouse they'd been renting in Toronto, Ontario, for five years. The office was located on the second floor of the house and all the windows were closed. The couple even played back the last few minutes of the video to make sure the sound didn't come from the show. It did not.

As they investigated the phantom hiss, George made a confession, prefaced with, "I don't want to freak you out, but..."

Four or five times over that previous year, on nights when Lynne worked the graveyard shift as a security guard, George had experienced a ghost cat.

The first time, while he laid in bed, an invisible cat head-butted his knee to get his attention. He looked, but Schrödinger wasn't around. Another time, he was awakened by a nudge that felt like a kitty hitting his foot. He only realized it was paranormal after he found Schrödinger in another part of the house.

Over the years, there were so many ghost cat encounters that the paranormal pet earned her own name, Spooky. Initially, neither Lynne nor George had a feel for Spooky's gender, but recently George has sensed the kitty is female.

George said on occasion, while he's lightly dozing, it feels like a cat jumps in bed with him. One night, he felt their new cat, Maddie, jump on the mattress next to him—or at least he thought it was her. He reached down to pet her but when he looked, surprise! Maddie, a dark tortoiseshell, was not on the bed.

On the night of their annual Day of the Dead party, Lynne finally had her own personal experience with Spooky—plus a paranormal bonus. After she went to bed, Lynne was having trouble falling asleep because she wasn't feeling well. Just as she dozed off, she felt a cat bump against her ankle, immediately followed by the blanket sliding off her foot. She looked, but there was no cat on the bed, or anything else. The ankle bump felt cat-like. The blanket action definitely wasn't. Annoyed, she pulled her foot back under the covers. A moment later, a deep male voice said in a normal speaking tone, "Luke." Her initial reaction was, "Are you kidding me? I was finally going back to sleep."

She also thought, "So I'm finally experiencing something, not just George now."

It's been ten years since the Day of the Dead party. They still haven't figured out who Luke was or who said it, and never heard that male voice again. They believe they have two distinct entities living with them: Spooky and a mischievous poltergeist they refer to as The Trickster.

The Trickster returns every few months to perform what George calls "weirdness." It makes things disappear and reappear in strange places. George's birth certificate vanished and then later turned up in an arbitrary drawer. Sometimes the poltergeist playfully touches the couple by poking them or tugging clothes in the kitchen or laundry room. Lynne describes it as significant but not threatening. On another occasion, the entity "mugged" Lynne while she was washing dishes. Suddenly, a cabinet door popped open and a coffee mug fell into the sink. A few years later, while George was out of town, Lynne was trying to read when the light kept flickering for no reason. The bulbs felt tight in the sockets and Lynne knew there hadn't been a power interruption because the television continued to broadcast. She yelled, "Knock it off!" and the flickering stopped.

"A lot of the activity is attention-seeking," she said.

Lynne and George decided to dust off their disused ghost-hunting equipment to try to capture evidence of their otherworldly tenants. While the video camera recorded upstairs in the living room, the couple checked out the basement. The upstairs camera captured no visually interesting evidence, but it did record a disembodied human sigh and the sound of something bumping the camera tripod.

Spooky is a less frequent visitor. She makes herself known a couple of times a year in different parts of the house. The interactions with the cat are always pleasant and attention-seeking, just like any normal, friendly cat, as if she's saying, "Hey, I'm here." Spooky's encounters are very brief—just long enough for a head bump and then she's gone. Periodically, they feel a cat brushing up against their legs. When they look down, there's no cat. Sometimes one of them spots what looks like a cat in the corner or somewhere else, but finds Schrödinger and Maddie in a different part of the house.

Whenever they experienced Spooky's head bumps, Lynne and George would check on their living cats and usually found them asleep in another part of the house. Spooky's head bumps are such a common occurrence, "We joke about having three cats," George said. "Spooky's a great third cat. We don't have to feed her or clean the litter box."

One year for Christmas, George gave Lynne a coffee mug with a drawing of a ghost on it. A note from Spooky apologized for scaring her. But truth be known, Spooky never frightened Lynne. Not even for a second.

After they added Maddie to the family, Lynne, who was alone in the basement doing laundry, bent over to load the dryer when she heard a younger cat meow behind her. She spun around, but there was no cat. The windows were closed and no one was in the courtyard outside the basement window. Checking upstairs, she found both cats sleeping on the top floor. She had no doubt the meowing cat was Spooky. Other than the *Ghost Adventures* hiss, it was the only ghostly feline vocalization they'd heard in the house.

Lynne said they have no idea who Spooky is or why she waited five years to engage with them. Schrödinger and Maddie are the only cats they've ever had. Their townhouse was built in 1969, and it's possible a previous tenant had a cat who passed away.

"Different kinds of weird things happen in the house," she said. "We usually attribute anything at cat level to Spooky, if the other two aren't in the immediate area. Some of the other stuff is definitely not Spooky and harder to explain." They don't know of any association between The Trickster and Spooky.

On occasion, the couple actually catches a glimpse of their ghost cat. Lynne thought she saw Schrödinger saunter down the basement stairs while she was doing laundry, but then actually saw him come down a couple of minutes later.

George has spotted Spooky in the poor lighting of the living room. Once, in the bedroom, Lynne spied a dark tail stroll by and caught a quick glimpse of orange cat eyes. Again, the only live suspects were in another part of the house. They could always hear their rather rotund corporeal cats thundering through the house or up the stairs on the hardwood flooring. This shadowy cat-shaped figure made no noise at all.

Although Spooky had been absent for a long time, the day Lynne and George were interviewed for *Ghost Cats 2*, she made herself known all evening long. George was preparing supper when he saw a cat in the front hall, then she vanished. He investigated, but once again it couldn't have been Schrödinger or Maddie. It had to be Spooky. Later that night Lynne was cleaning the kitchen and looked at a cat she saw on the staircase, and the cat vanished. Later, they were in the basement watching TV when Lynne saw a cat in the hall outside the TV room, then she was gone. Maddie and Schrödinger were playing in another part of the house. All three sightings that day involved a visible cat vanishing. Later, in the office where they first encountered Spooky, George saw a cat under his chair, but once again, their cats were not around. They believe Spooky heard Lynne and George talking about her and wanted to make her presence known.

Lynne and George don't really know if Schrödinger or Maddie ever react to Spooky. Sometimes they stare at nothing on the wall. Several times Maddie has jumped on the bed, looked at the ceiling, then fled the room as if something was after her. There was nothing there—or at least, nothing Lynne or George could see. Whenever Maddie and Schrödinger are acting weird, Lynne and George joke that they're playing with Spooky. If they hear a noise that sounds like a cat but isn't either of their corporeal kitties, they joke, "It must be Spooky."

About her paranormal boarders, Lynne said she likes the idea of having a ghost cat. She's not scared when The Trickster makes things happen around the house, although she sometimes gets pretty annoyed at some of his antics. She doesn't like staying in the house by herself at night. She won't go into the basement laundry room when she's alone at night. When George is out of town, she stays in the office upstairs after dark and avoids going beyond the kitchen. "It's not so much being scared as being uncomfortable with The

Trickster's annoying pranks," she said. "Maybe we should dig out our ghost hunting equipment and do another test run."

*****

Lynne and George live in Toronto, Canada, with their two corporeal cats, Madeline and Schrödinger.

Shadow Cat

Numerous generations of Gibbs have lived in their three-story brick home in southern Pennsylvania. Brady Gibbs's great grandparents built it in the late 1800s. Originally set out in the middle of nowhere, the home now sits within the concrete jungle that is York City, a community with early roots in the 1770s.

The three-unit complex has always been a part of Brady's life. His grandparents lived upstairs; his dad grew up on the first floor. After his grandparents moved, the second- and third-floor apartments were rented to numerous tenants over the years, many of them family.

With so much history, it's not surprising that some spirits continue to hang out in the century-and-a-half-old home.

For the longest time, a cat spirit roamed his apartment. Brady doesn't know who the ghost cat was, why it stayed, or what happened to it. He does know the ghost kitty was a tenant long before he became one. Brady moved into the second-floor apartment with his roommate, KitKat, an eight-year-old gray tabby he rescued from a highway median.

Within his first week in the apartment, Brady began having paranormal experiences. It started with weird noises—creaks and bumps. Later he began seeing things—little things, like a cat-sized shadow near the front door, backlit by the light from the stairwell. When he first noticed the little specter, he suspected it was KitKat, but in every case he found her sleeping soundly either at the foot of his bed or in her cat lounger. After a while, he stopped checking.

Sometimes out of the corner of his eye Brady caught a blur moving silently past the door. The shape reminded him of a cat lingering by the door, perhaps waiting for someone to let it out.

Every sighting has been in his peripheral vision—a brief movement caught out of the corner of his eye. If he looks directly at it, it vanishes. There are times when he's sitting on a chair watching television when he feels something brush up again his leg—the very distinct sensation of a friendly feline head bump—but when he reaches down to pet it or glances at his feet, there's nothing there. As a result, whenever he sees the ghost cat, he stays perfectly still so as not to frighten it away.

The image or touch is sometimes followed by chills and goosebumps—always afterward, never as a foreshadowing or as it's happening.

The shadow cat at the door never makes any noise, which Brady said is impossible. Those antique floorboards squeak and creak even when ten-pound KitKat treads across them. Any human-made noises from the upstairs tenants sounded like thundering elephants.

On rare occasions, Brady hears a faint meow in the distance—usually just one—sounding disturbingly like a trapped kitten. As always, at first he worried it was KitKat. And as always, when he investigates, KitKat is accounted for. After a thorough search of the apartment, there is no kitten to be found.

Brady has no idea who his extra feline roommate is. It may have belonged to one of his relatives or the other tenants who occupied the home. Only after he mentioned the ghost cat to his brother did Justin, who previously lived in the apartment for five years, admit he also had some crazy experiences there.

Justin, too, often saw a cat-sized shadow moving past the front door. He knew it wasn't his imagination. Justin's own cat, Storm, was usually in the room when he spied the shadow. Like KitKat, Storm often reacted to the presence as well. Frequently, Storm sat in the kitchen staring at the ceiling, his eyes sometimes tracking something invisible moving around the room.

KitKat works as Brady's paranormal detector; she confirms the things Brady hears and sees. More disturbing, she reacts to some things he can't detect. As with Justin's cat Storm, KitKat stands vigil in the kitchen, monitoring an invisible presence.

Sometimes at night, flesh-and-blood KitKat will suddenly dash back and forth through the house like a maniac. When it first happened, Brady just assumed KitKat was having a normal burst of the kitten crazies. Now he wonders if she's playing with the ghost cat or running away from something else.

Early on, Brady said the ghost cat appeared more frequently, but recently he hasn't seen it. He's not certain whether it has moved on or if Brady has become so used to the cat's presence that he no longer notices it. He has observed that the paranormal activity seems to increase in the fall, for some reason.

While Brady doesn't mind sharing his home with a ghost kitty, sometimes the apartment takes on an eerie feel. Brady admits the basement, with its musty dirt floor, is "kind of creepy." Even as an adult, he only descends the stairs into the cellar when he must.

Occasionally another unsettling entity joins Brady in the apartment, and there's nothing feline about it. Once, he felt someone (not a cat) lie beside him in bed. Brady was scared, but kept his eyes closed. He didn't want to see what or who was lying next to him. Whenever he turns off the lights, he backs away, fearing something or somebody may grab him from behind. At other times, he hears sounds as if someone human is moving around inside the apartment; it sounds heavy, like a person. On occasion, he hears the unmistakable echo of the front door latching. At night, he's heard the sound of a door being shut.

He has also felt someone touch his shoulder as he rocked in the rocking chair. He suspects that was his late mother, because he recognized her touch. He's also felt the presence of someone standing behind him. He slowly peers over his shoulder to find nothing.

Brady agrees with the Buddhist beliefs that we suffer in life and then die, and are reborn based on how we lived our life, in a long quest to find enlightenment. Whether human or animal, between death and rebirth some souls tend to hold on.

Smoky's Revelation

Sometimes cats bond with family members they've never lived with. After college, Elizabeth Cottam moved away from her parents' home in Mapleton, Oregon, to an apartment in Portland, where she worked as a workers' compensation claims examiner. On weekends or over the holidays, Elizabeth often made the three-hour drive to visit her mom and dad.

Five years after Elizabeth and her brother left home, and after their last cat passed away, Mom and Dad filled their empty nest by adopting two-year-old Smoky from the Florence Humane Society. Smoky was very affectionate, intelligent, and even though Elizabeth never lived with him, the two developed a very strong bond during her frequent trips home.

An impressive cat even in his youth, Smoky looked like a stocky Russian Blue, at one point weighing in at fourteen pounds. He had that soft silver-blue coat and green eyes the breed is known for. Russian Blues are also known as a socially shy breed, but Smoky was outgoing.

Smoky was a bit of an adventurer. He loved hanging out in his yard. He had his own cat flap in the back door to let him come and go as he pleased, at least during the day. (Smoky lost his evening door privileges when raccoons invaded the house in the middle of the night.) Nobody worried about Smoky. He always kept close to the house and away from the road.

While he had the massive bulk of a great hunter, it was all for show. If a mouse approached him begging to be killed, he obliged it, but he certainly didn't go out of his way to take it down.

During his outdoor adventures, he enjoyed basking in the sun. Afterward, he indulged in a dust bath, wiggling and rolling in the dirt and working it deeply into his fur. He always returned to the house wearing a second coat of fine silt. No matter where he slept, he left a gray, dusty ring of dirt behind.

He adored being around people and being petted. Whenever Elizabeth visited, Smoky could always be found by her side or on her lap. Unlike most kitties, Smoky loved belly rubs. Whenever he saw anyone, he flopped down in front of them, rolled fully onto his back, and stretched his front and back paws out to give them the best access. When he did this with Elizabeth, she dug her fingers deeply into his fur from his chin to his hips, back and forth. In response, he tipped his head back, squeezed his eyes shut, and purred. He didn't move a muscle and almost looked like he'd gone into a bliss coma.

Smoky especially liked it when Elizabeth donned one particular long, dark blue sweater. Whenever she wore it and sat on the floor, he snuck his entire body under the sweater behind her back and snuggled against her under it.

During those visits, Elizabeth slept on her side on the living room floor facing the fireplace, with her back to the room. Every night, Smoky started out sleeping with Elizabeth's dad, then in the morning, he quietly joined Elizabeth, stealthily snuggling down behind her knees. In the morning when she woke up, that's where she always found him.

After Elizabeth returned to Portland, Smoky wandered the house looking for her and calling for his absent buddy. To appease him between visits, whenever Elizabeth spoke with her mother on the phone, Mom put the phone down on Smoky's level so Elizabeth could talk to him. He'd get so excited to hear her voice that he'd head-butt and paw at the phone.

Then one afternoon, eight-year-old Smoky wandered into the road and was hit by a car. It was so unlike him to go in the street; the family never figured out why he did. Elizabeth's parents were devastated—so distraught they drove all the way to Portland to tell her in person that her feline friend died, a message they simply couldn't bear to deliver over the phone.

A couple of months later, Elizabeth was in bed in her apartment, lying on her side with her knees bent. Suddenly she felt the bed dip, as if a cat had jumped up on it. A moment later, she felt her rather stiff comforter mold down against the back of her knees. She lived alone; at the time she had no pets or roommates. A constant pressure leaned against the exact spot where Smoky liked to sleep. Carefully, without moving her legs, Elizabeth turned on the light. While she saw nothing, the comforter was still pressed against the back of her knees and stiffly tented away from her body everywhere else. After about ten minutes, the pressure disappeared and the comforter eased back up.

"I know that was Smoky visiting for a last time," Elizabeth said.

Elizabeth had mixed feelings about Smoky's visit. "Any contact again was so precious; I loved him so very deeply! But on the other hand, it was also a reminder that I would never see him or kiss him or rub him again."

Elizabeth told her parents about Smoky's visit. They agreed he had come by to say goodbye. Smoky had not visited her folks, at least, not they that they knew of. Elizabeth thought that was odd, because he loved them too. Mom, on the other hand, didn't seem surprised at all. She said that, given a choice, she knew Smoky would come back to visit Elizabeth in a heartbeat. Unfortunately, those fifteen minutes were their last together.

"I wish I could feel him again!" Elizabeth said. "I think he wanted one last time with me. He didn't get to see me as much as he wanted, so he wanted one more snuggle to hold him over."

Elizabeth also thought it was odd that specter Smoky dropped by, but her part Russian Blue, Silky, who had a closer bond with her, never visited after he passed.

"I really don't know why some come back and some don't," she said. "I do believe they will all be waiting for me though."

*****

Elizabeth is a lifelong cat lover, whose first full sentence was, "See the kitty!" She lives in western Oregon with two longhaired tuxedo twins, working from home in the middle of the woods, as any good (and lucky) hermit would.

Bedtime Visitation

Adam lived with his grandfather in a Victorian house with elegant vaulted ceilings and bay windows in New Mexico. Before long, he and Jenn married, and she joined them in the home. After Adam's ninety-year-old grandfather died, the newlyweds moved into his larger master bedroom.

It was just the two of them. No kids and no pets— at least not living animals. Their room had a California king size bed, long enough for Adam to stretch out and not hang off the end.

One night, about a year after they moved into the master bedroom, Jenn and Adam were lying in bed watching TV when the bedsprings gave as though something had pounced on the mattress. Tiny footsteps padded across the covers, then something settled down to nap between them.

Although they had no pets, the sensation felt familiar, routine, and so real they knew it wasn't a dream. At the same time, the couple turned to each other. In unison they asked, "Did you feel that?" What could it be but a ghost?

While Jenn wasn't terrified, she wasn't comfortable either. She'd grown up in a very religious family, so she avoided anything that might attract unfriendly entities. She said a prayer of protection aloud.

Over the next twelve months, the ghost cat visited five times. Often as they lay in bed, they felt the bedsprings dip, the pitter-patter of paws and something landing on the mattress. With every appearance of the ghost Jenn prayed, especially when she was alone.

Jenn often wondered about the identity of the ghost cat. Grandfather had only owned dogs. Growing up, Adam had a dog, but his sister had a cat. Their neighbor, who had lived next door her entire life, said an elderly couple lived there for a long time. Before they moved, in the 1960s the building was a drug house. When Adam's grandfather bought it, the realtor found strange writings inside the door of the linen closet. It took far more than the normal number of coats of paint to successfully mask the demented graffiti. People assumed someone had performed occult rituals in the house. Fortunately, the cat was the only entity present and its visits didn't cause a problem—until the last visit.

Adam worked the graveyard shift and often slept alone during the day. One afternoon, he was catching some sleep when he felt the fiery pain of something scratching his foot and biting his big toe. Cat lovers know that sensation, when Fluffy catches a hint of movement beneath the sheets, leaps into the air and clamps down on that enticing prey scurrying beneath the covers. There's the exquisite pain when claws and teeth contact the skin, the scream of agony, and the scurrying of paws as Fluffy dashes away.

Adam shouted and sat up in bed. Instantly, the attack stopped. Adam checked his foot; a tiny line of blood seeped from it. When Jenn returned home from work, Adam showed her the scratches. They raked the surface of his skin—typical cat scratches. Although the bloody foot scared Adam at first, they decided the cat meant no harm, but instead was simply a naughty cat who couldn't resist attacking whatever was moving beneath the bed covers.

After that, they switched bedrooms for a couple of months. When they moved back into grandfather's bedroom, the ghost cat never showed itself again.

They now live in a different home with five indoor rescue cats. With all those fur babies around, Adam said he feels like Captain Kirk drowning in tribbles. There's always something furry underfoot. The new house isn't without its mysteries, though. There are still times when all five cats suddenly lock eyes and simultaneously track something no human in the house can see. So who knows? Maybe the phantom feline is still with them; it's just learned better manners.

Marshmallow

Michelle Eyster and her husband, Jared, move from place to place—a lot. Jared works as a regional operations manager for a legal defense company, and whenever they need a new manager, Jared's their guy. In the past few years, they've lived in Pennsylvania, Wisconsin, and Indiana. In late October 2020, right before Halloween, they relocated again—this time to Virginia.

The Virginia move was a bit rushed, so Jared went apartment-hunting on his own and found a small two-story house townhouse he thought they'd both enjoy. The building was constructed in the early 2000s; it was so new that Michelle never imagined it could be haunted.

The move went smoothly. After all, Michelle and Jared are veterans at relocation. So are their pets. This was the third move for Kimber, a two-year-old chocolate Lab, and Theo (TT for short), their six-year-old light peach and white kitty with big green eyes. Since the two four-leggers are best friends, no matter where they move, there's always a familiar face in the new environment. They love to play with each other, and on occasion sleep and cuddle together.

When they first started unpacking, Michelle didn't feel anything out of the ordinary. After a few weeks of settling in, though, she noticed that her dynamic duo had uncharacteristically vanished during the day. She searched the place and found them hanging out in the upstairs bathroom. Standing back and watching, she noticed both animals took turns darting in and out of the bathroom, napping in there, and even frolicking. She found their behavior very odd. After all, the bathroom was so tiny that it didn't allow much space for play.

Their disappearance became a regular occurrence. After that, whenever Michelle lost track of them, she almost always found them in their bathroom getaway. They seemed to feel safe and happy there. While their behavior was odd, she didn't think much of it. Anyone who has a cat knows they tend to hang out in very strange places. And Kimber liked to goof off near his feline friend.

In late November, Michelle discovered the reason for the pets' fascination with the room. During the wee hours of the night, she got up to go to the bathroom. As soon as she walked out of the bedroom, through bleary eyes she spied a bright white cat sitting on the floor just outside the bathroom door. The cat didn't move from that spot in the corner. It glowed brightly from within; Michelle said it was almost as if she was looking at a cat-shaped light bulb. It certainly wasn't a reflection off of any light inside the house.

Michelle thought it was weird, but she was only half awake and her vision was blurry from sleepiness. As she approached the cat, it appeared to scurry into the bathroom, then vanish into thin air, like a cloud of smoke.

That first night, she thought she had just seen TT. However, when she went back to the bedroom, he was sound asleep on her pillow. "What was that in the hallway?" she wondered. But she shrugged it off and slipped back into bed, never having completely awakened.

The following night on her late-night bathroom run she once again encountered the glowing white cat in the hall. And, as had happened the previous night, TT was snoring on her pillow. Even though she knew it wasn't TT, she didn't immediately jump to the possibility it was ghost. The nightly pattern continued. It took her a couple more sightings before Michelle realized she'd experienced a ghost kitty.

Michelle became so fond of her little ghost cat, after encountering him almost every night for two weeks, that she decided to give him the name Marshmallow. She calls the little spirit "him" because she gets male vibes when she's around him. Although Marshmallow didn't loiter in the hallway every night, Michelle usually encountered the translucent cat a couple of times a week—always when the hall was dark. The more she saw it, the less it vanished upon her approach.

Suddenly everything made sense. She understood why TT and Kimber loved the upstairs hall near the bathroom. Marshmallow made it an area that felt happy and safe.

Although she felt fine with the presence of the ghost cat, the feeling wasn't immediately mutual. Like many cats, it took a while to build his trust. After Michelle encountered him five days in a row, the specter finally stopped vanishing upon her approach. It took about a month for him to stop completely disappearing. With each encounter, he remained visible in the hall for longer and longer periods. Sometimes he scurried into the bathroom with Michelle. If she turned on the light, he vanished.

The ghost was real, but she didn't want to say anything to Jared—not yet. Finally, when she spotted Marshmallow for four nights in a row, it was time to come clean about her ghost sightings. At first, Jared thought Michelle was joking, but when he figured out she was serious, he told her he would keep an eye out when he went to the bathroom at night.

About a week after Michelle's confession, Jared came upon Marshmallow. He got up in the middle of the night and clearly saw Marshmallow sitting outside the bedroom door. When the ghost kitty noticed him, the little spirit dashed into the bathroom. Michelle awoke to find the hall light on and Jared pacing up and down the hallway looking for the cat. He finally blurted out, "It's real."

Michelle let out a sigh of relief. Now that Jared had seen the ghost kitty, she knew she wasn't crazy. "I got so happy and excited to see him at night," she said. "Marshmallow gave me a feeling of peace and safety, like a security blanket; he made me feel protected." She started looking forward to seeing their little third pet.

Marshmallow has been a protective spirit for TT as well. They adopted TT from a shelter in Wisconsin in 2018. The shelter worker told them that the then-three-year-old cat had been found on the streets, emaciated. Splattered black tar clung to his fur throughout his coat. Some human beast had shot him in the neck with a BB gun. Not surprisingly, everything frightened him: loud noises, people, nothing, and everything. To complicate matters, he was under-socialized; for the first couple years he didn't trust anyone—a broken spirit, so to speak. By the time Michelle and Jared moved to Virginia, he weighed thirteen pounds. TT snuggled up next to Michelle's head every night. Things were certainly better, but he was still broken.

Since moving in with Marshmallow, it's like someone flipped on TT's happy switch. He's now playful and loving; he meows and struts around unafraid. Jared said Marshmallow's presence explains why TT and Kimber have been so vocal and playful lately.

"I love my little ghost kitty," Michelle said. "I figured Marshmallow saw how loving and caring I was to my other animals and he wanted some love too.

Marshmallow is now a full-fledged member of the family. Michelle occasionally puts toys and treats outside of the bathroom for him. She doesn't know if Marshmallow ever plays with the toys. So far, none of them have moved on their own.

Michelle sees Marshmallow every night now. He no longer runs away or vanishes when she approaches. He even solicits her attention. Early one morning, she saw him and, believing he was TT, she extended her hand the same way you let a cat or dog sniff it. Marshmallow reached out, as if trying to rub his head against her. Her hand swished through his white, glowing form. She felt no sensation of touch or fur. Then, "clear as day," he sat down next to her feet and looked up into her eyes. His eyes appeared like big black marbles. They may have a color, but Michelle has yet to see it.

"It's becoming such a normal thing that it's just part of my routine now," Michelle said. "I feel very comfortable and happy with him being here. What's better than having a ghost cat as a pet? I don't have to clean out the litter box or pay for vet visits!"

They do worry about Marshmallow, since another move is eventually inevitable. "We are currently looking to buy here in Virginia, not too far away," Michelle said. "I'm sad that I'll leave my ghost pet behind, but I'm also hopeful there's a way he can come with us. If not, I hope he enjoys the next people who move in just as much as he loves showing up for us!"

The Black Cat

Keep Austin Weird. Everyone in Texas knows that is the motto of Austin, the Lone Star State's capitol. Weird just comes with the territory.

Maybe it shouldn't have been a surprise when weird things started happening in Sheri and Tim Ray's new house in Cedar Park, a suburb of Austin. They bought the ten-year-old house in 1994 and lived in it briefly before taking a job out-of-state. For five years, they rented it to a family with no pets. They returned to the house in 1999 with their two Persian cats, a black boy named Yeltsin, and Tugger, a tortoiseshell girl.

Sheri isn't really a cat person, but Tim is. He grew up with Persians. As long as they have been together, they've always had at least one or two Persians around. Sheri's fine with the cats, with one condition: Cats don't sleep in the bedroom with them. She's a very light sleeper and can't go back to sleep after being awakened by the nocturnal imps.

Just a few months after moving back to Cedar Park, Tim was away on a business trip. Sheri went to bed around eleven, as usual. About three in the morning, Sheri was awakened by a cat jumping on her.

"Okay," she said as she turned on the bedside lamp, "Which one of you snuck into the room before I shut the door?" She glanced down at the floor just in time to see a black tail disappear under the bed.

"All right, come on up here." She sat up and patted the bed; that usually brought them running to get pets, but the cat remained hidden. She grabbed one of Tim's belts and dangled it over the side of the mattress. Neither of their kitties could resist that wiggling, snaky prey. Uncharacteristically, neither Yeltsin nor Tugger leaped for the bait. Something else was going on. Sheri checked on her two suspects, but the Persians were sleeping together on the couch in the living room.

Back in her bedroom, she sat on the edge of the bed and thought about her experience. Nothing made sense. The mystery cat's tail had short, sleek, black fur, not a fluffy Persian tail. She checked under the bed just to make sure a stray cat hadn't somehow sneaked into the house. No kitty. Had there really been a feline intruder, her own pets would have made enough noise to raise the dead.

Finally she told the cat aloud, "I don't mind you being here, Kitty, but please don't jump on the bed in the night. It wakes me up and I have trouble falling back to sleep." She slid back into bed and turned off the light. Honoring her request, the ghost kitty never appeared in the bedroom again.

Over the next three years, both Sheri and Tim caught glimpses of a sleek black cat in different places around the house: the living room, the hall between the master bedroom and the living room, the kitchen. They most often saw the cat either sitting smack in the middle of the living room, its tail primly wrapped around its front feet, or coming out of the master bedroom and sauntering down the hall toward the front door. Sometimes they caught a glimpse of its tail as it slunk around a corner into another room.

Lying in the middle of the floor, it appeared as solid as a normal cat. It was medium size, compact, with a roundish head. It had a shiny, slick, black coat, a long tail, and yellow eyes. Neither Sheri nor Tim had a feeling for whether it was a girl or boy ghost. Time of day didn't seem to matter to the ghost kitty; it materialized day or night, whenever the mood struck it.

The ghost cat appeared to be aware of them, but didn't seem to be afraid or upset when they walked into the room. It usually hung around for just a moment or two. They'd catch a glimpse of it, but when they turned back to look again, it would be gone. Sometimes it watched family members but moved away or vanished if someone tried to approach it. If they ignored it, it stayed around longer. The living room sightings lasted a bit longer, as well. On occasion, they'd laugh and remind it not to go into the bedroom at night.

Over the next three years, the couple saw the ghost cat about twenty times. The black kitty even showed itself to guests. One guest returned from the bathroom with a funny little smile on her face. "You don't have a black cat, do you?" It was more a statement than a question. Sheri said, "Oh, you saw the black cat?" She had seen it disappear into the back bedroom. She followed it, but when she got to the room, there was no cat.

While the ghost cat reacted to the humans in the house, the Persian cats didn't respond to its presence at all.

Neither Sheri nor Tim had a clue who the little kitty was. All of Tim's past cats were Persians with dense, long coats. Sheri's mom had a black cat when Sheri was born, but he had a small white spot on his chest and this cat was solid black.

They wondered if the cat had belonged to a previous owner of the house but they had no way to find out. Whoever the ghost kitty was, he obviously belonged there.

In 2011, the Rays sold the house and moved to Austin proper. The day they moved, Sheri sat in the bedroom one last time and told the ghost cat it was welcome to come with them.

Sheri doesn't know if it couldn't leave or wouldn't leave, but after they moved they never saw the black ghost cat again. Sheri said they were both sad the little ghost didn't join them. She often wonders if the people who bought their house ever caught a glimpse of a sleek black feline ghost.

*****

Sheri Graner Ray is a veteran computer game designer, author, and speaker on the subject of games and game design. Her website is www.SheriGranerRay.com

"Are you my Mommy?"

CHAPTER 6: POSSESSED POSSESSIONS

Death, well done, is a gateway from this world into another. It needn't be the end of anything. —Stephanie Dray

Any object that has been handled repeatedly has the potential to hold a spiritual imprint. Physical objects act like sponges, absorbing the energy of repeated touching and handling. Over time, a possession can store the quintessence or character of its owner, which lingers as a kind of psychic recording. A person later handling the object may receive feelings and mental impressions about the people or pet who once used the item.

Holding a haunted object may give you a happy or invigorated feeling or an uneasy sensation, depending on the energy left behind and the type of haunting: residual or intelligent.

In a residual haunting, the object acts as a spiritual sponge, and with repeated use, it retains layers of the user's energy. An item may become haunted because of someone's emotional attachment to it. A cat toy may hold energy from many happy hours of playing with a beloved person, or a figurine may absorb the grief of a human whose cat passed away. The energy acts like a video recording; it plays back the feelings or experiences, but there's no intelligent action.

Then there's the intelligent haunting, in which a personality actively responds to people or situations. Intelligently haunted objects may house the spirits of pets or people who have died under dramatic and tragic circumstances, or spirits who, for whatever reason, aren't ready to move on. The object may vocalize or move around on its own or emit a scent.

I had mixed feelings about including stories about haunted cat-related possessions in this book, primarily because of the potential to bring in a negative energy or spirit attached to an object. Spirits and entities looking for a non-corporeal home seem drawn to antiques and older items. The energy attached to that cat statue or doll may never have been feline or human. You don't want to welcome something antagonistic, or worse, into your home. Evicting a negative entity may not be as easy as throwing the haunted item away, so buyer beware.

There's also an entire cottage industry of cat-related merchandise with supernatural attributes—everything from cat figurines and statues to jewelry, artwork, cat toys, food bowls, and even haunted collars. You can buy anything on the Internet, from a cat butt tissue holder to LED light saber chopsticks to an infectious disease coloring book. Why not a cat ghost?

Online merchants of the paranormal can't simply sell an empty envelope containing a disembodied ghost cat. Marketplaces such as eBay, Etsy, and Craigslist require sellers to provide either a physical item or a tangible service. Entrepreneurs therefore offer objects a ghost or entity is attached to, not the ghost itself.

Any claims made about these objects are difficult to verify. Consequently, sellers must run a disclaimer that says something like, "As required per eBay's policy on the sale of paranormal items, this is for the sale of a tangible item only, no promise of a spirit attached"; eBay items listed as haunted or possessed are offered "for entertainment purposes only."

No matter which shopping platform you use, there are usually "buyer beware" warnings—along with warnings of hazards associated with an impending paranormal presence in your home. With all the charlatans out there trying to make an easy buck on people who want a paranormal experience, "caveat emptor" could not be more appropriate.

Did you buy an object and nothing happened? Sellers claim

haunted objects aren't like buying a cell phone that works for anyone. They say just because the resident spirit moved around or spoke to the previous owner of the object doesn't mean the same will happen with the new buyer. If nothing happens, sellers say maybe the spirit doesn't feel that love connection.

My advice to you is enjoy Fluffy's cat toy that occasionally moves on its own, or the food bowl that sometimes meows or the cat collar that jingles. But beware buying haunted items online. Most likely, you're buying a worthless piece of garage sale junk. And if you do end up with the rare object that is truly possessed, you may be welcoming something that is unfriendly and definitely not feline.

In Raisa's Image

Skye doesn't remember much about her Great-Grandma Zofia, but she recalls her as a serious woman, plump and round, who always wore a scarf over her hair, no matter where she was or whether the temperature was twenty degrees or one hundred. She remembers curly strands of white bangs peeking out from beneath her head covering. Skye's memories were sketchy, so she didn't know if her mental images of Zofia were real or if she was pulling up imagined memories from often-repeated stories she'd heard as a child.

Before the first shots of World War II were fired, Zofia's son and daughter-in-law immigrated to the United States, and Zofia and her husband stayed behind on their small farm in the southern part of Poland. Her husband was killed in the German invasion, leaving Zofia alone with only her black cat, Raisa. While Zofia had many barn cats, and loved them all, Raisa not only kept the rodent population inside the family farmhouse at bay, but also kept the widow company. Raisa loved to hunt and often brought Zofia trophies from her expeditions. With no veterinary care available, Raisa lived a short life, only a few years. But in that time, she won Zofia's heart, as well as killed hundreds of rats.

Toward the end of World War II, Zofia escaped occupied Poland and joined her family in the United States. She didn't take much with her on her journey to her new life: a few sets of clothes, a tattered photo of her husband, and a porcelain black and white cat figurine her husband had given her.

Skye remembers meeting Great Grandma Zofia only once. By that time, the elderly babushka was a hunched and shriveled woman. She remembers how bony Zofia's knees felt when she sat on her great-grandma's lap. Zofia handed Skye the porcelain cat and instructed Skye to take good care of it for her. Babushka called it Raisa. It was all she had left from the old country.

Skye didn't really understand what her babushka gave her. Her parents had only kept dogs, and at the time Skye thought the figure was simply a dog with pointy ears. Skye grew up and moved from home, but always kept Raisa with her. Long after Great-Grandma had left this life, Skye continued to treasure her gift.

At some point, Skye began seeing a disembodied shadow hanging around the statue. It was a translucent black cat with a long, flowing tail. At first, she saw brief glimpses of the cat, lasting only a fraction of a second. Over time, the cat stayed visible for up to ten seconds. The ghost cat never strayed more than a foot away from the figurine. Finally, when the ghost cat appeared, Skye grabbed her cell phone and took a photo. The dark cat figure appeared directly behind the porcelain cat. She could clearly make out the details of the rounded head, pointed ears, even a tail snaking out from behind. A thin, shadowy tail, like that of a rat, drooped from where the shadow cat's mouth should be. The phantom cat had caught a phantom rat. When Skye showed her mother the photo, Mom knew it had to be the spirit of the black cat from Zofia's farm in Poland.

Skye still only has dogs, and her Labrador Retriever mix, Boomer, often stares, fixated, at the cat figurine. Sometimes he growls. Sometimes he raises his hackles. Boomer's just going to have to learn to get along with Zofia's ghost kitty. She's not going anywhere.

Chunk's Friendly Vet Toy

Chunk was Cynthia Broussard's twenty-three-pound gelatinous ball of tabby fur who was prone to projectile vomiting and bladder infections. In his more than two decades with Cynthia, the humongous tabby never once raised a claw in anger. He loved to eat, sleep, snack, nap, and check his food bowl between meals. He could also play fetch for seemingly hours at a time with his favorite toy, a Friendly Veterinarian catnip-filled doll. The toy's catnip had long since lost its attraction. It had been thrown, carried, and dropped so many times that the seams were unraveling. Sean, the kid next door, frequently came over to play fetch with Chunk, a sort of toss-till-you-drop event. Chunk never seemed to tire of the game, even with a boy filled with pre-teen energy.

Although Chunk was the life of the party, Cynthia's new stepdaughter, Hannah, was less than thrilled about having to visit her dad in the presence of a cat. Hannah's mom was an admitted ailurophobe and transferred her fear of cats to her four-year-old daughter. Eventually, Chunk somewhat won Hannah over. She occasionally played fetch with him in the long hallway to her bedroom.

Between his immense size and the arthritis that accompanied his many but happy years, Chunk hadn't been able to jump on Larry and Cynthia's bed for years. Instead, he slept on an old pillow in the corner of their bedroom.

Sadly, at the age of twenty-one, Chunk's body stopped working. Suddenly, the family was one being smaller. Cynthia donated Chunk's bed and food to a local rescue group, but she couldn't bear to let go of the Friendly Vet toy. It lay on the floor next to the sofa—the place he'd dropped it at the end of his last game of fetch.

The night after Chunk's passing, Larry woke up to intense pressure on his chest—the kind of pressure Larry had heard accompanies heart attacks. As he sat up in bed, the sensation vanished, but immediately Cynthia screamed as she felt a cat scramble across her body and leap down from the bed. She even had a couple of fine scratches across her upper arm, as if a cat had used her shoulder as a launching pad.

They turned on the light but found nothing in the room.

"You think that was Chunk?" she asked Larry.

He nodded. There was no other explanation.

Although Cynthia and Larry were broken-hearted over Chunk's passing, Hannah took it calmly, and maybe with some relief. However, the next time she visited her dad, she saw the supersized specter in the living room near his Friendly Vet toy. Later, Hannah found the Friendly Vet on the other side of the room, and then later in the day, in the hall.

Larry explained that if it really was Chunk's ghost, he would be a friendly presence, just as he was friendly in life—think Casper the Friendly Ghost. Hannah could have a pet and not have to take on any care chores. But nothing Larry said could convince Hannah she was safe in a house with a ghost. She refused to go to their house for visits.

Finally, Cynthia came up with a plan. She gave the toy to Sean. Problem solved. Hannah stopped seeing Chunk. Sean reported no paranormal activity at his home. Apparently, Chunk had moved on.

"Our room is ready."

CHAPTER 7: GHOST CAT TRAVEL GUIDE

A cat is only technically an animal, being divine. —Robert Lynd

Some hotels have amazing vistas of the nearby mountains or ocean waves lapping against a beautiful beach. Others offer a variety of adventures and activities that you'll remember for the rest of your life. Some hotels have cats who work as pest control officers or in guest relations.

Just as some hotel rooms have prior guests who never checked out, in some cases the hotel cat continues to hang around long after he has tackled his last rodent. These kitties no longer hunt mice—at least not live ones—but they'll jump on your bed and snuggle up with you.

Over the years I've discovered some fascinating hotels and bed & breakfasts that readily admit to having permanent pets. Here are a few you might enjoy visiting.

Jerome, Arizona

Jerome, in central Arizona, sprang up during the copper-mining boom in the late 1800s. The town sits on the side of the mountains, more than 5,000 feet above the Verde Valley, between Sedona and Prescott.

In the late 19th century, the United Verde Copper Company opened a lucrative mine that extracted copper, gold, and silver ores. Where miners went, bars, brothels, hotels, opium dens, and pool halls quickly followed. The picturesque mountainside was transformed into a thriving community. In its heyday in the 1920s, Jerome was home to more than 10,000 people.

The need for copper fluctuated throughout the town's history, but when the ore deposits ran out in the 1950s, the mines closed. Jerome's once-thriving population had dwindled to fifty—a ghost town, literally and figuratively.

Today, boutiques, art galleries, and coffee houses have replaced the brothels and opium dens, but there are still hotels and bars that offer a place to spend the night or order a cold one. This recently reinvigorated ghost town has a thriving paranormal population, including several hotels with ghost cats.

Jerome Grand Hotel
200 Hill St.
Jerome, AZ 86331
jeromegrandhotel.net
888-817-6788
928-634-8200

The historic Jerome Grand Hotel originally operated as United Verde Hospital. Opening in January 1927, it was the fourth medical facility built in Jerome by the United Verde Copper Company to care for its miners and their families.

The 30,000-square-foot hospital provided cutting-edge (for the time) medical care. Built in the Mission Revival Style of architecture, it was built of poured-in-place concrete. Not only was it fireproof, it was designed to be earthquake-proof, a necessity because it rested on the side of Cleopatra Hill and needed to withstand frequent dynamite blasts from the nearby mine.

Considered the most modern hospital in Arizona at the time, it boasted an Otis self-service elevator that served all five floors, patient call lights, emergency backup lighting, an ice-making room, laboratories, X-ray machines, operating rooms, blanket-warming closets, and separate wards for men, women, and children. It also had balconies and therapeutic sun porches. Being the highest commercial building in the Verde Valley, it offered a spectacular view (and still does.)

United Verde Hospital closed in 1950 as the copper ran out and the mine began to shut down. The building stood abandoned and boarded-up for the next forty-four years. In 1994, it was purchased by Larry Altherr, who transformed it into the Jerome Grand Hotel. The hotel opened for business in 1996. Larry Altherr still owns the full-service boutique hotel.

Sarah Moser, Jerome Grand Hotel general manager, said the hotel wants to be recognized as a historic hotel rather than a haunted hotel, so they don't actively promote the presence of the ghosts. However, they acknowledge that they do have permanent guests (two- and four-legged.)

Moser said, "Cats have been reported throughout the building, even in the lobby, which was the hospital's emergency room, and the boiler room. Most often, the cat is located on the second and third floors. Rooms 20, 26, 28A, and on the third floor in the corridor and rooms 32 and 39A and the Grand Suite are common areas where the cats are felt, heard, smelled and photographed. A bearded miner can also be seen wandering the halls and sometimes children can be heard giggling. A ghost dog can also be seen from time to time."

Guests have described different cats in the hotel journals. Some have seen longhaired felines. Others describe shorthaired kitties. The colors and markings vary as well. Staff doesn't know if guests are seeing one cat that appears differently to various individuals, or different ghost cats.

A recent guest shared her encounter with one of the hotel's permanent pets. Cindy Adams from Hudsonville, Michigan, knows you only live once, and spending the night at a haunted hotel was on her bucket list. In March 2016, while attending her daughter's national college softball tournament in Tucson, Cindy set up a side trip to the haunted town of Jerome, Arizona, to fulfill her paranormal passion.

En route to Jerome, she received a voicemail from the Jerome Grand Hotel informing her that the evening's ghost tour had been canceled. To make up for the disappointment, the manager upgraded their room to one of the hotel's most active rooms for ghostly encounters, Room 20. Suddenly disappointment turned to fear. A haunted hotel was one thing, but a haunted room . . .

While Cindy and her husband, Jim, were checking in, a hotel employee offered to take the couple on a private hotel ghost tour. That night the guide handed Cindy and Jim a temperature gauge and an electromagnetic field meter and showed them how to use them. She took the couple from floor to floor, showing them all the rooms and common areas where most of the ghost encounters occur. During the tour, she mentioned that after people have gone to bed, they often hear doors opening and closing.

As they heard the stories, Cindy wondered, "Oh, my goodness! What have I gotten us into?" She said, "By the time we got done with the tour, I was petrified. I wanted to check out of the hotel but I didn't know where else we would go."

When they retired to their room that night, Cindy was terrified. Suddenly that bucket list dream seemed more like a nightmare. Before they went to bed, she held her husband's hand and prayed out loud for protection. Cindy fell into a troubled sleep.

After going to bed, Cindy heard the doors opening and closing. Jim heard it too. He said it was just people entering their rooms. After dozing off, Cindy was awakened by something soft and feathery brushing across her face. Not daring to open her eyes for fear of what she might see, she squeezed them tightly shut. She turned over to face the opposite direction. A few moments later, she once again felt fuzzy softness stroke her face. She never summoned the courage to take a peek. "I was a scaredy cat indeed!" Cindy admits.

The next morning, before they checked out, she went to the lobby and read several of the guest journals describing encounters with the unknown. One of the books contained a photograph of a beautiful cat sitting on a bedside table. She looked closer at the photo; the cat appeared transparent. The clerk acknowledged the hotel does indeed have a resident cat ghost that had been photographed by numerous guests.

In retrospect, Cindy realized she had nothing to fear from her nighttime visitor. Instead of being approached by a miner or a murdered security guard, she recognized the soft thing that stroked her face was the fluffy fur of a longhaired ghost cat.

"It was a chilling experience," Cindy said. "But if I was going to be haunted by an entity, I much prefer the meowy kind. If you get the chance and are brave of heart, I recommend a stay there."

The Clinkscale Hotel
309 Main Street
Jerome, AZ 86331
theclinkscale.com
928-634-5094

The six-room Clinkscale Hotel has existed under different names and types of businesses for more than 120 years. Built in 1899, it was originally occupied by J.J. Clinkscale's hardware store. At that time, the street level housed shops and the upstairs rooms were rented as apartments.

The fireproof Clinkscale Building replaced wooden structures that were destroyed by three fires that devastated the town in the late 19th century. The new structure at 309 Main Street was fireproof, with eighteen-inch-thick walls made of poured, reinforced concrete.

For a while, the building housed a bordello run by Jennie Banters. Legend has it that Madam Jennie still haunts the hotel, as does her cat. Other versions of the legend claim the female ghosts who reside at the hotel are an older woman and her cat who lived in the wooden building when it burned down in 1897.

The hotel was formerly known as the Mile-High Inn. After a recent change of ownership, the structure was renamed The Clinkscale Hotel and Restaurant and the business renovated to add modern amenities. The Clinkscale offers six guest rooms, all located upstairs. Haunted rooms include the Pillow Talk Room and the Spooks, Ghosts, and Goblins Room.

Evidence of the ghost cat is seen throughout the building, and it is often heard meowing around two or three in the morning.

Noah Rivera, assistant manager of the hotel and restaurant, said he experienced the ghost cat once. When he was first hired, the manager allowed him to stay in the Pillow Talk Room. For just a moment, he saw a form low to the floor that reminded him of a cat. After he went to sleep, he felt a small animal jump on the bed. He described the action as "soft and gentle."

"It felt like one of my cats had jumped on the bed. It was a gentle feeling. I thought, 'This is cool.'"

Noah has worked there for about eighteen months, but so far this has been his only paranormal experience.

Hotel management doesn't want the hotel to be known only for its paranormal residents, but they don't deny their presence, either.

Employees, guests, and paranormal investigators have reported a wide variety of ghost cat activity, including the apparition of a cat walking through the halls, a friendly feline rubbing against their legs, and the sound of a cat grooming its claws. A cook claimed to have witnessed a cat strolling through the kitchen and then disappearing. The invisible cat also takes naps in different rooms, leaving cat-shaped indentations on the beds. As one guest described it, "It looked like someone plopped right down in the middle of the bed."

DO YOU HAVE AN ANIMAL GHOST STORY TO SHARE?

The boundaries which divide Life from Death are at best shadowy and vague. Who shall say where the one ends, and where the other begins?
—Edgar Allan Poe

Did you enjoy *Ghost Cats 2*? Have you had an experience with any animal ghost that you would like to share? The animal doesn't have to be your own; maybe you've stayed in a hotel haunted by a dog or a cat? Could you hear the clip-clop of hooves as you approached the front door of the hotel? Maybe you've seen the shadows of horses on an old battleground.

Dusty expects to follow up *Ghost Cats 2* with *Ghost Cats 3*, as well as editions dedicated to *Ghost Dogs, Ghost Horses,* and *Ghost Pets* (for animals that don't fit into feline, canine, or equine categories.)

Share your story with Dusty Rainbolt by emailing her at ghoster@pobox.com. You must include your name, email address, and phone number, and be available for either email or telephone interviews.

If Dusty uses your encounter in an upcoming book, she'll send you a paperback copy.

ABOUT THE AUTHOR

Dusty Rainbolt is an award-winning cat writer, according to her answering machine. She has worked as a professional freelance journalist since the late 1980s, and began specializing in feline health and behavior in 1995. She is the author of *Cat Scene Investigator: Solve Your Cat's Litter Box Mystery*, an award-winning book that helps cat owners rectify their cat's litter box mishaps. Her books also include *Ghost Cats: Human Encounters with Feline Spirits; Kittens for Dummies; Finding Your Lost Cat: The Practical Cat-Specific Guide to Your Happy Reunion;* and *Cat Wrangling Made Easy: Maintaining Peace & Sanity in Your Multicat Home*.

She also penned the paranormal mystery, *Death Under the Crescent Moon*. Her sci-fi fans know Dusty for her comedy novel *All the Marbles*, as well as the outrageous *The Four Redheads of the Apocalypse* fantasy series she co-wrote with Linda L. Donahue, Rhonda Eudaly, and Julia S. Mandala. She's past president of the Cat Writers' Association, and three-time recipient of the Friskies Writer of the Year award and recipient of more than sixty writing awards for her articles, books, and columns on feline health and behavior.

She and her husband share their unhaunted home with their living, breathing cats. Involved in kitten rescue for more than three-and-a-half decades, she has fostered and rehomed more than 2,500 cats and kittens, including more than 1,500 surviving orphan kittens.

Unfortunately, not all of the bottle babies made it. One in particular changed her life. A former card-carrying skeptic, Dusty started investigating paranormal phenomena after her recently passed foster kitten named Maynard returned for a brief one-time afterlife experience.

Check out Dusty's website at www.dustycatwriter.com and her publisher www.StupidGravityPress.com. She'd love to hear your cat, dog, and horse ghost stories.

GHOST CATS 2

www.ingramcontent.com/pod-product-compliance
Lightning Source LLC
Chambersburg PA
CBHW022007120526
44592CB00034B/628